A CATALOGUE
OF THE COLLECTION OF
PERSIAN MANUSCRIPTS

A CATALOGUE

OF THE COLLECTION OF

PERSIAN MANUSCRIPTS

INCLUDING ALSO SOME TURKISH AND ARABIC

PRESENTED TO THE

METROPOLITAN MUSEUM OF ART

NEW YORK

ALEXANDER SMITH COCHRAN

PREPARED AND EDITED BY

A. V. WILLIAMS JACKSON

AND

ABRAHAM YOHANNAN

GYAN

Published by

GYAN

Gyan Publishing House
5, Ansari Road
Daryaganj, New Delhi-110002
Phone: 011-47034999, 9811692060
E-mail: books@gyanbooks.com

Distribution Network
gyanbooks.com
India, USA, Canada, UK, Australia, France

ISBN: 978-81-212-8364-9 (PB)
First Published, 1914

2nd Impression 2023

Printed at: Gyan Press, Delhi.

A CATALOGUE OF THE COLLECTION OF PERSIAN MANUSCRIPTS
Author: ALEXANDER SMITH COCHRAN, EDITOR: A. V. WILLIAMS JACKSON, ABRAHAM YOHANNAN

A CATALOGUE

OF A COLLECTION OF

PERSIAN MANUSCRIPTS

A CATALOGUE

OF THE COLLECTION OF

PERSIAN MANUSCRIPTS

INCLUDING ALSO SOME TURKISH AND ARABIC

PRESENTED TO THE

METROPOLITAN MUSEUM OF ART
NEW YORK

BY

ALEXANDER SMITH COCHRAN

PREPARED AND EDITED BY

A. V. WILLIAMS JACKSON
PROFESSOR OF INDO-IRANIAN LANGUAGES

AND

ABRAHAM YOHANNAN
LECTURER IN ORIENTAL LANGUAGES, COLUMBIA UNIVERSITY

New York
COLUMBIA UNIVERSITY PRESS
1914

Bibliographical Note

Seven volumes of the Indo-Iranian Series have been previously published (volumes 2–8, 1901–1913; see the announcement following page 187). As the *Sanskrit Grammar for Beginners*, heretofore announced as the first volume of the Series, is not yet ready for publication (though nearly complete in manuscript), the present work is, for general convenience, issued as Volume 1 in its stead.

Set up and electrotyped. Printed February, 1914.

Norwood Press
J. S. Cushing Co. — Berwick & Smith Co.
Norwood, Mass., U.S.A.

PREFACE

THE preparation of this catalogue has been a pleasant task during the past two years, though the appearance of the work has been considerably delayed by the many exactions of university duties. The plan followed in describing the manuscripts was originally adopted in conference with Mr. Cochran while he was collecting them for his own library, and now that he has presented the collection to the Metropolitan Museum of Art in New York City in order to make it accessible to the public, the plan then designed seems equally suitable for the purpose of the general exhibition of the collection.

The descriptive method, thus chosen, has kept several objects in view. By the side of technical matters for the information of Oriental specialists, particular attention has been paid to the art side of the collection, so as to convey some idea of the illuminations, miniatures, bindings, and the like, in addition to matters of literary interest, details of historic import, or items of a personal nature regarding the individual owners of the copies in generations long past, as gathered from the Oriental seals and memorandums. It would seem that no serious objection could be raised critically to the fulness with which such matters are recorded in the pages that follow.

To the generous donor who made the manuscripts accessible to the public and available to scholars that may wish to consult them in future, a special acknowledgment is due. Beyond that, a personal expression of thanks is owing to him for the constant interest that he has shown, in every possible manner, in the preparation and publication of the catalogue. Without his aid the volume could not have appeared in the Columbia University Indo-Iranian Series.

Words of appreciation are likewise due to Mr. Frederic W. Erb, Mr. Frank Erb, and Miss Adele Erb, of the Library Staff at Columbia, as well as to the Librarian of the University, Dr. W. Dawson Johnston, for obliging assistance in connection with the handling of the manuscripts during the year and a half that they were deposited in the Columbia University Library vaults for consultation in the preparation of this catalogue. In like manner Director Edward Robinson and his assistant, Mr. Henry W. Kent, of the Metropolitan Museum, together with Curator W. R. Valentiner and Mr. D. Friedley, have been equally kind in granting every possible facility in consulting the codexes since they have been on public exhibition in the Persian room at the Museum. Nor is to be forgotten the help they gave while the illustrative plates were being prepared, so as to convey an idea of some of the miniatures that adorn the collection.

Among other friends who gladly lent aid may be mentioned Professor Richard Gottheil, of Columbia University, who gave assistance in connection with certain points relating to the Qur'ān and other important matters. As to valued suggestions concerning the character and quality of the paper in the different manuscripts, acknowledgment is also made to Mr. Douglas C. McMurtrie, of New York. There is an appropriate opportunity here, furthermore, to thank Miss Susan Yohannan and Miss Cassandra Yohannan for their untiring work in copying and re-copying each section of the book as it was being prepared for the press.

Last but not least, that friend, student, and faithful helper, Dr. George C. O. Haas, sometime Fellow in Indo-Iranian Languages at Columbia and now Instructor in the College of the City of New York, deserves a very special acknowledgment; he not only prepared the Index to this work, but also gave readily, as usual, his technical advice in all matters relating to the make-up of the volume and his skilled service in reading every revise of the proofsheets, to supplement the care bestowed by the readers of the Norwood Press.

To each and all of these willing helpers most hearty thanks are expressed anew.

A. V. WILLIAMS JACKSON,
ABRAHAM YOHANNAN.

COLUMBIA UNIVERSITY,
July 1, 1913.

CONTENTS

LIST OF ILLUSTRATIONS

LIST OF WORKS OF REFERENCE

This list includes the works most often cited, together with those that may profitably be consulted in connection with this catalogue. Details regarding other books and papers are given in the body of the work.

Amīr Khusrau of Delhi. For bibliographical references see Ethé, Neupersische Litteratur, in *Grundriss der iranischen Philologie*, 2. 245.

Beale, T. W. Oriental Biographical Dictionary. New ed., London, 1894.

Blochet, E. Les Écoles de peinture en Perse. In *Revue archéologique*, 4. sér. 6. 121–148, Paris, 1905.

—— Les Miniaturistes des manuscrits musulmans. In *Gazette des beaux-arts*, 39. année, 3. période, 17. 281–296; 18. 104–118, Paris, 1897.

—— Les Origines de la peinture en Perse. In *Gazette des beaux-arts*, 47. année, 3. période, 34. 115–130, Paris, 1905.

—— Peintures de manuscrits arabes, persans et turcs de la Bibliothèque Nationale. Paris, [1911].

Browne, Edward G. A Literary History of Persia. 2 vols., London and New York, 1902, 1906.

—— Catalogue of the Persian Manuscripts in the Library of the University of Cambridge. Cambridge, 1896.

D'Allemagne, Henry-René. Du Khorassan au pays des Backhtiaris: compte rendu. Paris, 1911.

Elliot, Sir H. M. The History of India as told by its own Historians: the Muhammadan Period. Edited by Professor John Dowson. 8 vols., London, 1867–1877.

Ethé, Hermann. Neupersische Litteratur. In *Grundriss der iranischen Philologie*, 2. 212–368, Strassburg, 1896–1904.

Firdausī. Firdusii Liber Regum qui inscribitur Shah Name, ed. J. A. Vullers (et S. Landauer). 3 vols., Leiden, 1877–1884.

——The Shāhnāma of Firdausī, done into English by A. G. and E. Warner. Vols. 1–6, London, 1905–1912.

——Le Livre des rois, traduit et commenté par Jules Mohl. 7 vols., Paris, 1876–1878.

——Il Libro dei re, poema epico, recato dal persiano in versi italiani da Italo Pizzi. 8 vols., Turin, 1886–1888.

Gayet, A. J. L'Art persan. Paris, 1895.

Grundriss der iranischen Philologie, herausgegeben von Wilhelm Geiger und Ernst Kuhn. 2 vols., Strassburg, 1895–1904.

Ḥāfiẓ. See the works referred to on page 128.

Havell, E. B. Indian Sculpture and Painting illustrated by Typical Masterpieces, with an Explanation of their Motives and Ideals. London, 1908.

Horn, Paul. Geschichte der persischen Litteratur. Leipzig, 1901.

Huart, C. Les Calligraphes et les miniaturistes de l'Orient musulman. Paris, 1908.

Jalāl ad-Dīn Rūmī. See the works referred to on page 94.

Jāmī. See the works referred to on page 139.

Karabacek, J. Über das angebliche Bilderverbot des Islams. In *Kunst und Gewerbe*, 10. 281–283, 289–291, 297–299, 307–308, 315–317, 332–333. Nuremberg, 1876.

Mahler, Eduard. Chronologische Vergleichungstabellen, nebst einer Anleitung zu den Grundzügen der Chronologie. Vol. 1, Vienna, 1889.

Manucci, Nicolao. Storia do Mogor, or Mogul India, translated by G. W. Irvine. 4 vols., London, 1906.

<**Martin, F. R.** The Miniature Painting and Painters of Persia, India, and Turkey from the eighth to the eighteenth Century. 2 vols., London, 1912. (This invaluable work became accessible only after the 'copy' of the present volume was ready for the press; information drawn from it has been inclosed in angular brackets< >to indicate its subsequent addition.)>

Mīr 'Alī Shīr Nawā'ī. See the works referred to on page 159.

Muqtadir, M. A., [and **Ross, E. D.**]. Catalogue of the Arabic and Persian Manuscripts in the Oriental Public Library at Bankipore. 3 vols., Calcutta, 1908–1912.

Niẓāmī. See the works referred to on page 48.

Pertsch, W. Verzeichniss der persischen Handschriften der königlichen Bibliothek zu Berlin. Berlin, 1888.

Rieu, C. Catalogue of the Persian Manuscripts in the British Museum. 3 vols., London, 1879–1883.

—— Supplement to the preceding. London, 1895.

—— Catalogue of the Turkish Manuscripts in the British Museum. London, 1888.

Rūmī, Jalāl ad-Dīn. See the works referred to on page 94.

Sachau, E., and Ethé, H. Catalogue of the Persian, Turkish, Hindūstānī, and Pushtū Manuscripts in the Bodleian Library. Part 1, Oxford, 1889.

Sa'dī. See the works referred to on page 101.

Saladin, H., et Migeon, G. Manuel d'Art musulman. 2 vols., Paris, 1907.

Sarre, F. Rizā 'Abbāsī, ein persischer Miniaturmaler. In *Kunst und Künstler*, 10. Jahrgang, Berlin, 1910.

Sarre, F., und Martin, F. R. Die Ausstellung von Meisterwerken muhammedanischer Kunst in München, 1910. 3 vols., Munich, 1912.

Shāh-nāmah. See Firdausī.

<**Valentiner, W. R.** The Cochran Collection of Persian Manuscripts. In *Bulletin of the Metropolitan Museum of Art*, 8. 80–86, New York, 1913. (A brief announcement of the gift of the collection, illustrated by three plates of selected miniatures, which are reproduced in this volume, thanks to the courtesy of the Museum authorities.)>

LIST OF ABBREVIATIONS

A.H. . . . *Anno Hegirae*, Muḥammadan Era.
Bull. . . . Bulletin.
c. . . . *circa*, about.
Cat. . . . Catalogue.
ch. . . . chapter.
cm. . . . centimeter, centimeters.
col. . . . column.
d. . . . died.
ed. . . . edition, edited by.
fl. . . . . *floruit*, flourished.
fol. . . . folio.
Hss. . . . Handschriften.
in. . . . inch, inches.
l. . . . line.
n. . . . note.
op. cit. . . *opus citatum*, the work previously cited.
pl. . . . plate.
tr. . . . translation, translated by.

< > . . . Angle brackets indicate that the matter so inclosed is based on published material by Martin or by Valentiner that became accessible after the 'copy' of this volume was ready for the press.

INTRODUCTION

THIS collection of Oriental manuscripts — twenty of them Persian, two Eastern Turkish, and two Arabic — was presented to the Metropolitan Museum of Art in March, 1913, by Mr. Alexander Smith Cochran, of Yonkers, New York. All of the codexes are handsomely illuminated and are adorned with beautiful miniatures, the entire collection containing much that is of interest to students of art, literature, and history. A number of the manuscripts are in certain respects unique.[1]

Mr. Cochran's interest in Persia was first aroused by a journey he made through that country six years ago in company with his friend, the Editor of this volume. Shortly after his return to New York he enriched the Museum by the gift of an extremely rare Persian rug, which may now be seen displayed in one of the galleries, not far from the Morgan collection of paintings. His present donation of manuscripts fills four large cases occupying the greater part of the Persian room that adjoins the latter collection.[2]

[1] The general points of this whole Introduction, which describes the main features of the collection, have previously appeared in an article by A. V. W. J. entitled 'Persian Manuscripts' in *The Nation* (New York), 96. 627–628, June 19, 1913.

[2] Prior to this gift the Metropolitan Museum of Art possessed only one Persian manuscript, a copy of Sa'dī's *Būstān*, together with a selected collection of manuscript pages with ornamental borders, as specimens of Persian decorative art, and a number of single-leaf paintings, not from manuscripts, by the artists Sulṭān Muḥammad, Riḍā 'Abbāsī, and Qāsim.

The manuscript of the *Būstān* is a fine copy, comprising 139 folios and

Persian illuminated manuscripts are growing rarer every year, as connoisseurs and collectors well know, and are ever increasing in value because of the exquisite miniatures with which the finer ones are adorned. In this realm and in the line of artistic embellishment Persia was able, four and five centuries ago, to produce specimens of art that have never been equaled elsewhere in their particular way. The Persian scribes, moreover, were unrivaled masters of calligraphy, because the art of beautiful handwriting was cultivated as one of the highest of refined accomplishments. The bindings, likewise, in which the Persians chose to clothe the work of their best writers were often masterpieces of workmanship.

It is true that for a time Persia had to borrow from China certain elements, including grace of line and other features, that were to be developed further with subtle skill by Mongol artists in Transoxiana and Turkistān; but she made all of these her special property in the realm of art. She was prepared in turn

embellished by five full-page miniatures in addition to other rich ornamentations. The copy has a partly obliterated colophon in two lines. In this the name of Mīr 'Alī al-Ḥusainī can be deciphered with some difficulty as that of the scribe, the date being given as 929 (?) A.H. = 1522–1523 (?) A.D. This date is fully corroborated by the general style and especially by the handwriting of the scribe, which appears to be identical with the penmanship of the renowned calligraphist Mīr 'Alī, who in 1523–1524 A.D. transcribed the copy of Jāmī's *Yūsuf and Zulaikhā* in the Cochran collection (No. 18, see p. 147–148 below), and it is borne out likewise by the style of the miniatures, which may well be attributed to Shaikh-zādah Maḥmūd of Khurāsān, chief artist at the court of the Shaibānid princes of Transoxiana at this period. <See especially W. R. Valentiner, *Bulletin of the Metropolitan Museum of Art*, 8. 80, whose deductions are based on Martin, *The Miniature Painting and Painters of Persia, India, and Turkey*, 1. 55, 116–117, London, 1912; and compare Huart, *Les Calligraphes et les miniaturistes de l'Orient musulman*, p. 331, Paris, 1908.>

(Attention may be called here to the fact that the angular brackets < > used throughout this catalogue indicate matter included from, or based upon, published material by Martin or by Valentiner that became available after the 'copy' of this volume was ready to go to press.)

to hand to Mughal India her refined gifts which made the artists at the courts of the Emperors Akbar, Jahāngīr, Shāh Jahān, and Aurangzīb the greatest portrait miniaturists of the world. The studies of such scholars as the French critics Blochet and Huart, the German authority Sarre, and the Scandinavian expert Martin, whose standard work on the miniature paintings of Persia, India, and Turkey was published a few months ago in two splendid volumes, render possible a truer judgment of the worth of the present fine collection. Detailed references to all these works are made in the Bibliography below and also in the body of the volume.

From the standpoint of literature, before turning to the artistic side of the collection, it may be noted that this valuable body of codexes represents the works of the greatest Persian classic writers. There are five different manuscripts (Nos. 1–5) of the famous epic of Firdausī, who flourished about 1000 A.D. Six manuscripts (Nos. 6–11) contain the entire works of Niẓāmī or parts of the writings of that celebrated romantic poet of Persia, who died about the year 1203. Next Jalāl ad-Dīn Rūmī (1207–1275), renowned above all in the East as *the* Persian mystic poet, is represented by a volume (No. 12) copied two centuries after his death and well worthy of note. Then Sa'dī (about 1184–1291 A.D.), the centenarian poet and moralist whose name is certainly better known in the Orient outside of his country than that of any other Persian author, claims two fine illustrated and illuminated volumes (Nos. 13–14). The Indo-Persian poet Amir Khusrau of Delhī, who won well-deserved fame in Hindustān in the thirteenth century through his recastings of Niẓāmī's romantic types, is represented by a beautiful little book (No. 15), dating from the time of the last of the Mughal emperors and bearing witness, by its exquisite paintings and finish, to the reverence in which this Persian-Indian bard was held — a reverence that can best be appreciated by the few Westerners who have paid a visit to his tomb near Delhī. Persia's far-famed lyrist Ḥāfiẓ, in the fifteenth century, one of the great musical poets in all literature, has five hundred and more odes incorporated in a small manuscript (No. 16), delicately outlined by ornamental flowerets and adorned by small miniatures to illustrate the subjects of the poems. The works of Jāmī, the last classic poet of Persia, the year of whose death corresponds with the date of the discovery of America, are here in four manuscripts (Nos. 17–20), one of which (No. 17) is peculiarly valuable, as it belongs to Jāmī's own lifetime.

Outside the realm of Persian works, there are two very rare illuminated and illustrated manuscripts in Jaghatā'ī Turkish, the language of Eastern Turkistān (Nos. 21–22). They both contain lyric works of the laureate-minister and poet-statesman Mīr 'Alī Shīr Nawā'ī, who died in 1501 after a renowned career at the court of Herāt in Afghānistān prior to the founding of the empire of the Mughals in Hindustān, and whose fame lasts in the East even to the present time through his poetry. One of the copies in this collection (No. 21) was transcribed a year or two before his death; we can imagine the interest that it must have had for courtier friends.

No collection belonging to the Muslim realm of Persia, Central Asia, and the adjacent domains would be complete without a fine copy of the Qur'ān. The oldest manuscript in the Cochran collection is a specially valuable specimen of the Muḥammadan scriptures in two volumes (Nos. 23–24), completed on June 29, 1427, which was transcribed by Tamerlane's grandson, Ibrāhīm Sulṭān, son of Shāh Rukh and brother of the famous royal bibliophile Bāisunghar. To illustrate the Sacred Word by pictures would be against the spirit of Islām, but exquisite ornamentation might be lent to the text itself in the form of chaste embellishment, especially to grace a copy of the Qur'ān transcribed by a prince's hand. Not only is this copy written by a prince and beautifully adorned, but it has the further distinction that it descended through the line of the great Mughal rulers

Similarly in the *Yogavasis'tha Maha-Ramayana* it is said that for the purposes of true adoration there is no necessity of incense, lamp, flower, sandal, and similar other external objects.

At first worship appears very painful and troublesome to one who is not used to it and who has not acquired true faith. But if a man strictly adheres to it, and steadfastly practises it, he is sure to experience its sweetness when the difference between his individual soul and the Universal Soul is washed away. He then finds that the pure and sweet pleasure of Divine meditation has no peer in this world. The real Swâttik pleasure consists in worship, prayer and divine meditation. It may be painful in the beginning, but it is very sweet in the end. The Lord Krishna thus describes it in the Divine Lay:

"Swâttik happiness is that in which one finds pleasure from repetition of enjoyment, which brings an end to all pain, which is like hungry, one should always worship the Great Soul with a purified mind. Who should, O Kuleshâni, take refuge under any other than Him, Whose worship does not either require any toil, fast or bodily labour; nor any restriction, the profuse provision of articles, distinction of time or direction, Mudrâ or Nyâsa.*

---

* वाचिकं कायिकं वापि मानसं वा यथामति ।
आराधने परेशस्य भावशुद्धिर्विधीयते ॥
अस्नातो वा कृतस्नानो भुक्तो वापि बुभुक्षितः ।
पूजयेत्परमात्मानं सदा निर्म्मलमानसः ॥

Mahanirvana Tantra., Chap. III., V. 75—78.

नायासो नोपवासश्च कायक्लेशो न विद्यते ।
नैवाचारादिनियमो नोपचाराश्च भूरिशः ॥
न दिक्कालविचारोऽस्ति न मुद्रान्याससंहतिः ।
यदाराधने कुलेशानि तं विना कोऽन्यमाश्रयेत् ॥

Ibid, Chap. II., V. 52—54.

Vide Author's English Translation.

till it reached Aurangzīb, the last of these emperors in India. On the back of the last leaf he records the history of the copy and the date when he made the memorandum of his reading it, in 1638 A.D., more than two centuries after the manuscript had been transcribed. He was then a prince in his nineteenth year and had not yet sat upon the throne. The court gilder embellished the pages with brush-work of ornamental gold around Aurangzīb's handwriting.

A remarkably precious manuscript of the *Haft Paikar* of Niẓāmī (No. 5), containing a romantic epopee on the subject of the Sāsānian king Bahrām Gūr ('that Great Hunter'), who reigned in the fifth century of our era, furnishes not only a cherished transcript of a master-work, but formed a gift fit for a king, as it was presented to Akbar the Great by a grandee whom he had appointed to be governor in the Panjāb. A regal memorandum in a painted medallion on the first page records that it was offered as a special tribute to the sovereign. The year of the gift was 1580, at which time we know that Akbar was at Lahore in the Panjāb. The imperial seal and other memorandums attest the fact of presentation and prove the royal ownership; and we know from court records that the works of Niẓāmī were among the emperor's favorite reading. The volume descended to his grandson, Shāh Jahān the Magnificent, as shown by an official signet. But the manuscript has an additional value and interest, since it contains five rare miniatures by Bahzād, the most famous of all Persian painters, whose death occurred about fifty years before. The miniatures are all genuine, each being signed in the authentic minute handwriting of Bahzād, which — as was characteristic of him — was so fine that a microscope is needed to decipher the name.

The artistic value of the collection has been indicated already, and we may be sure that books which formed part of the libraries of Oriental potentates, as shown by seals and memorandums, were choice copies. The finest in the entire set is a magnificent manuscript (No. 8) of the works of Niẓāmī, transcribed by the famous calligraphist Sulṭān Muḥammad Nūr, who completed the transcript in the year 1525. This superb codex, which is sumptuously embellished, came from the library of the Ṣafavid kings of Persia and was among the treasures of the later Shāhs. It is written on heavy, gold-frosted paper, with a different marginal color to distinguish each of the five long romantic poems, and is incased in the original flap-cover, which is a specimen of rare beauty in the way of binding. But beauteous above all are the fifteen miniatures with which it is adorned. They are from the brush of Mīrak, the celebrated pupil of Bahzād, and the most famous of all Persian artists after his master. < Regarding this manuscript Dr. Martin writes in terms of the highest praise when he says (1. 116): 'It is second to none of the same period; there are certainly larger ones in existence, but none of finer quality with such a profusion of architecture and such charming coloring.'> The views of the seven different palaces in which Prince Bahrām Gūr visits the seven princesses, his wives from the seven realms of the world, are particularly notable. < Of the artistic treatment of these themes Dr. W. R. Valentiner, of the Metropolitan Museum, says (*Bulletin of the Metropolitan Museum of Art*, 8. 86): 'These subjects, which demand a different color-scheme for each miniature to correspond with the different colors of the palaces, black, yellow, green, and so forth, have always been among the favorite problems of the Persian painters, but never has higher decorative value been given to these manuscripts than by Mīrak in this Niẓāmī, in which the hue of the walls in the different palaces is the motive upon which is built up an exquisite symphony of color.'>

There are points of art to admire in other manuscripts of the set. We may note, for example, the expression of the faces, so remarkably caught in miniature, in a seventeenth-century copy (No. 14) of a Persian classic, Sa'dī's *Būstān*, or 'Garden of Perfume,' which belonged to the library of Shāh Jahān and that of his son Aurangzīb. The borders of its pages, with extra-decorated insets, are unusually ornate; and it is interesting to observe from the well-worn condition of this copy, with its sixteen official seal-impressions and memorandums, how extensively it was read at the court.

Another manuscript of special value (No. 17), more than a hundred and fifty years older than the preceding, as its date is not far from 1465, is one of the four copies of Jāmī's poems in this collection, transcribed a quarter of a century before his death. It is a *Dīwān,* or select volume of his lyric and mystic verses, and, besides being richly illuminated, is adorned with sixteen beautiful miniatures, which show strongly the influence of Mongol art and are important for the study of the art of painting at that time.

The art of calligraphy by the side of miniature painting may be illustrated by still another copy of Jāmī (No. 18), transcribed by the illustrious penman Mīr 'Alī in 1523 and 1524; also by one of the copies (No. 21) of the poems of Mīr 'Alī Shīr Nawā'ī, which was copied in 1500 by the hand of the renowned 'Alī Mashhadī.

Imperfect as is this account, it would be still more lacking if some notice were not taken of a special variety of art, shown by five of the manuscripts, in portraying scenes from Firdausī's *Shāh-nāmah,* Persia's great national epic, composed nearly a thousand years ago. Students of literature are familiar with the tragic episode of Suhrāb and Rustam through Matthew Arnold's adaptation of the story of the unknown heroic son who is unwittingly slain in single combat by his warrior father, Rustam. Art connoisseurs will scan with interest the delineations of this fearful scene as drawn by the different artists. Nor will any critic of the brush overlook, among other miniatures, one by 'Alī Naqī in a seventeenth-century copy of the *Shāh-nāmah* (No. 4, fol. 24*b*). In this picture the artist depicts the grief of King Farīdūn, who, somewhat after the manner of Gorboduc or distantly like Lear, has divided his realm among his three sons, and, in consequence of the bloody internecine strife that arose among them, receives on a golden salver the head of his youngest and best beloved son, slain by the elder brothers. Only a great miniaturist could so perfectly convey the poet's conception of a parent's heartrending sorrow.

Allusion has previously been made to the lovely little manuscript, bound in red leather, of the Delhī poet Amīr Khusrau, as an example of Indian-Persian miniature art (No. 15). It dates from the time of the last of the Mughal emperors, Aurangzīb, the hero of Dryden's drama, whose grandsire, Jahāngīr, the 'Great Mogul,' boasted of a knowledge of technique in art that could distinguish if a different brush gave the concluding finish to an eyebrow in a portrait.[1] The delicacy of touch in the miniatures of this particular manuscript bears witness to the nonpareil of workmanship attained by the several artists at Aurangzīb's court who have affixed their signatures to the paintings.

In addition to the manuscripts themselves must be mentioned a series of twenty-nine single-page paintings of the seventeenth and eighteenth centuries, most of which are not drawn from manuscripts, but were specially prepared as examples of art. Five of these are in the Persian style of Riḍā 'Abbāsī. Among those from India, dating from the Mughal period, may be mentioned a fine portrait of the Emperor Jahāngīr, another painting in which he is depicted as reverently paying his respects to a pious dervish, and still a third which represents in splendid style his son Shāh Jahān, mounted on horseback. < Dr. Martin chose two of these to be among the six which he selected for reproduction in color in his second volume (vol. 2, pl. D, p. 79; pl. E, p. 87).> The Cochran set contains four-

[1] See E. B. Havell, *Indian Sculpture and Painting*, p. 199, London, 1908.

teen other single-sheet paintings in the Indian style, and also seven beautiful specimens of Persian calligraphy.

Enough has been said to show the artistic, literary, and historic importance of the collection, the details regarding which may be gathered from the descriptions of the separate manuscripts in the ensuing pages.

PERSIAN MANUSCRIPTS

I

FIRDAUSĪ

PERSIAN MANUSCRIPTS

FIRDAUSĪ

(about 935–1025 A.D.)

PERSIA's celebrated epic poet, Firdausī, author of the *Shāh-nāmah*, or 'Book of Kings,' a work which ranks among the great epics of the world, was born about 935 A.D. in the ancient city of Ṭūs, whose ruins are still to be seen a few miles distant from Mashhad in Northeastern Persia. By descent he belonged to the landed gentry of Īrān and had, therefore, an inherited interest in his country's great past.

For fully thirty-five years, or from about 974 to 1010, Firdausī worked upon his famous epic, a poem of nearly sixty thousand couplets. Much of it he composed at the court of the great conqueror Maḥmūd of Ghaznī, in Afghānistān, a patron who ill rewarded his labors and who was consequently held up to scorn by the poet in a satire as immortal as the epic itself. Fleeing from the monarch's wrath he found himself, at the age of seventy-five, a wanderer without proper means of support; but ultimately he received shelter at the court of a minor Persian ruler in Ṭabaristān, where he composed a notable long romantic poem, *Yūsuf and Zulaikhā*, on the love of Potiphar's wife for Joseph, as recorded in the Qur'ān after the Bible. Returning at last to Ṭūs, Firdausī died in his native city at an advanced age in 1020 or 1025 A.D.

The *Shāh-nāmah* is a poetic chronicle based upon older prose annals, now mostly lost. It portrays the national history of Īrān from the age of the mythical ruler, Kaiūmarṣ, or Gayūmart, whom tradition places about 3600 B.C., down to the death of the last Sāsānian King, the historic Yazdagard III, in 641 A.D., and the events directly preceding the fall of the empire before the Arabs.

The main stages of the epic, so fully illustrated by the paintings in the present collection of *Shāh-nāmah* manuscripts, are as follows: After beginning with the primeval ruler Kaiūmarṣ, the poem describes the kingship of Hūshang, who was the discoverer of fire, of Tahmūrāsp, 'the binder of demons,' and of Jamshīd, sovereign of the golden age. A foreign usurper, Ḍaḥḥāk, or Zahāk, representing the tyrannical rule of Babylon and Arabia over Persia, seized the throne and reigned for a legendary period of a thousand years. The power of this monster was destroyed at last by a national hero of Īrān, the noble Farīdūn, only to be followed by an internecine strife between the deliverer's three sons, Īraj, Tūr, and Salm, who succeeded respectively to the kingdoms of Persia, Tūrān, and China. Īraj was slain by his two brothers. This deed of blood started the inveterate warfare between Īrān and Tūrān, which forms the burden of a large part of the epic. King Minūchihr ultimately mounted the throne of Īrān; a romantic episode then tells of valiant Zāl, whose love for Rūdābah gave birth to a son, Rustam, the hero of the epic. Rustam's martial exploits, herculean labors, and signal triumphs (one being even the tragic slaying in battle of his own son Suhrāb, whom he did not know) run almost to the end of the poem. Kings follow kings in the order preserved by tradition until the rise of the Prophet Zoroaster, some three centuries before the invasion of Alexander the Great. The appearance of this ancient prophet gives occasion for chronicling the reign of his patron, King Gushtāsp, and the latter's son, Asfandiār, crusader for the faith, as well as for recounting the religious wars between Īrān and Tūrān, still more embittered by the difference of creed. The latter part of this reign of the Kaiānian kings corresponds with the close of the great Achaemenian empire of Persia; and at this point the rimed chronicle begins to pass from the realm of legend into the domain of history. The overthrow of the Kaiānians was brought about by the invasion of Alexander the Great, followed by the assassination of Darius III (Dārā) in 330 B. C. The epic narrative compresses the next five hundred years, or the empire of the Parthian Arsacids, into the briefest possible summary of the events of half that period. A historic account in general of the Sāsānian rule, from 226 A.D. to about the year 650, offers a special opportunity to record, among other reigns, that of Bahrām Gūr, as well as that of Nūshīrwān the Just, and the epic brings the story down to the murder of Yazdagard III (in 641 A.D.), the last king of Īrān before Persia was conquered by the Muḥammadan Arabs.

Abundant material is accessible in the way of editions and translations of the *Shāh-nāmah*, as shown by the bibliographical citations in the exhaustive treatise by Th. Nöldeke, *Das iranische Nationalepos*, in Geiger and

Kuhn's *Grundriss der iranischen Philologie*, 2. 130–211. For other details regarding Firdausī's life and work see E. G. Browne, *Literary History of Persia*, 2. 129–147, London and New York, 1906; P. Horn, *Persische Litteratur*, p. 81–114, Leipzig, 1901; E. A. Reed, *Persian Literature*, p. 214–283, Chicago, 1893. There is an abridgment of the *Shāh-nāmah* in English by J. and J. A. Atkinson (London and New York, 1886) and by A. Rogers (London, 1907), and an English translation into blank verse by A. G. and E. Warner (London, 1905–); a translation into French by J. Mohl (Paris, 1876–1878), and into Italian by I. Pizzi (Turin, 1886–1888).

1

Firdausī (c. 935–1025 A.D.): **Shāh-nāmah.**—A large illuminated and handsomely illustrated manuscript of the great Persian epic poem *Shāh-nāmah*, or 'Book of Kings,' carrying the narrative down to the death of Alexander, with which event the codex ends. It contains the close of a Preface, the first pages of which are missing. The manuscript belongs to the latter part of the sixteenth century (being dated 1587–1588 A.D.), and contains forty large miniatures in addition to the two illustrations on the inside of the lacquer covers.

Size. — Height and width, $15\frac{1}{2} \times 11$ in. (39.5×28.0 cm.). Height and width of written page, $12 \times 7\frac{1}{2}$ in. (30.5×19 cm.). Folios 596, comprising roughly about 49,000 couplets. A leaf between folios 1 and 2 is missing.

Binding. — Beautiful lacquer binding (though not the original covers) with a golden yellow background exquisitely adorned with delicate flowered designs on the outside and decorated by two large illustrative scenes on the inside. The illustration on the inside of the front cover represents a meeting between two kings who are seated in state, surrounded by their attendants, while officers of the army are stationed in review before them. The illustration on the inside of the back cover represents a king under a canopy in a garden; his attendants are around him and a suppliant kneels in obeisance before him. The manuscript has been subjected to a rebinding and to a trimming of the pages, which gives the copy a neat appearance, but has unfortunately resulted in cropping some of the folios too closely, so that a part of many of the catchwords at the bottom of the right-hand pages has been cut off, the top of the illuminated title-pieces has been slightly clipped, and the figure of a man on the margin of fol. 49*a* has been almost trimmed off.

Writing and Paper. — Large clear Nastaʿlīq hand, 21 lines to the page in four columns with marginal rulings of blue, red, and green. The paper is of a light creamish tint, of medium sheen, pure-laid on a rather cross screen; it is of fairly constant composition and of a comparatively light weight.

Date and Scribe. — The date of the manuscript (1587–1588 A.D.) and the name of the copyist, Shāh Muḥammad of Sabzavār, are both given. The scribe's name is first recorded on fol. 161*a*, at the end of the first of the four subdivisions into which the codex is divided, as follows: 'The (first) book is finished with God's help by the humblest Shāh Muḥammad of Sabzavār, the scribe.' The date itself with the scribe's name is given at the end of the manuscript in the colophon on fol. 596*a*: 'Finished by the hand of the most humble Shāh Muḥammad of Sabzavār, the scribe (may God forgive him !), in the year 996 A. H. [= 1587–1588 A.D.].' The district of Sabzavār is in Khurāsān, north-eastern Persia, between Teherān and Mashhad.

Memorandums. — There are seal impressions stamped on several folios (fol. 1*a*, 177*a*, 327*a*, 331*a*, 417*a*, and 596*a*). The oval one on fol. 1*a* is the signet of Muḥammad Saif ad-Dīn, the date in the body of this seal being 1200 A.H. = 1785 A.D. The octagonal seals on folios 1*a*, 327*a*, and 596*a* are identical with each other, but in them only the name 'Muḥammad' can be deciphered. The square seal on fol. 177*a*, which is surmounted by a triangular crown, is not legible, but above it are written, in an inverted order as in a seal, the figures for 1222 (A.H. = 1807 A.D.) and the words *ba ism*, 'in the name of' (likewise half in inverted order.) Above this there are two or three words, not quite distinct, but *mushīr*, 'minister,' is legible. In two spaces in the body of the text near this seal there is twice written in a bold hand in Persian 'Shăh [*sic*] Zādah Yūnis.' The oval seal on 417*a* is not legible, but appears to differ from the oval one on fol. 1*a*; above it are written in inverted order as in a seal the figure 1222 (A.H. = 1807 A.D.) and the words *ba ism* likewise half inverted as in a seal, as in the case of that on fol. 177*a*; and above it the figures for '11.' On folios 331*a* and 396*a* are the marks of a little square seal, but illegible. There is the impression of a third large square seal on fol. 596*a*, but it has been erased. On the margins of several pages are explanations of Persian words or more modern terms for the ones that are comparatively obsolete.

Subject and Arrangement. — The epic history of Persia down to the death of Alexander the Great. The codex contains a portion of the so-called 'Older Preface,' often prefixed to the manuscripts of the poem (cf. Rieu, *Cat. Pers. Mss. in British Museum*, p. 534), but the first part of this is unfortunately missing down to the list of kings with the traditional length of their respective reigns, the list here beginning only with the Sāsānian monarchs Hurmazd I, son of Shāpūr I, followed by Bahrām and the rest. The poem itself opens on fol. 1*b* with the lines

بنام خداوند جان وخرد کزین بر تر اندیشه بر نگذرد

The manuscript is divided into four unequal parts or divisions, each of which is introduced by an illuminated 'unwān, or title-piece, as follows: (*a*) Close of a Preface, fol. 1*a*. — I (fol. 1*b*–161*a*). First part of the epic. — II (fol. 161*b*–446*a*). 'Book of Kai Khusrau.' — III (fol. 446*b*–556*a*). 'Book of Bahman.' — IV (fol. 556*b*–596*a*). 'Book of Alexander.'

Illuminations and Illustrations. — The manuscript is illuminated by four richly adorned 'unwāns, or title-pieces, as introductions to the four books or subdivisions that have been mentioned, each of these ornate titles occupying a third of the page. The ever recurring captions or head-bands to the different sections of the poem are written throughout in white ink upon a gold background and occupy the space of two distichs between the two middle columns; the band, however, on fol. 1*b*, is blank, but was doubtless intended for extra decorations because it heads the section relating to the praise of wisdom; the writing is missing in the gold band in fol. 348*b*. As an additional embellishment to the body of the text the verses preceding the miniatures, or in some cases both preceding and following a miniature, are written in small square spaces delicately adorned with floweret designs of a violet and reddish color — a feature found in other manuscripts as well. Besides the two illustrations on the inside of the lacquer covers, described above, under Binding, there are forty full-page miniatures to illustrate the text. These all appear to be the work of a single artist and are markedly Mongolian-Persian in style. The figures as a rule are rather large, boldly drawn, without overmuch attention given to minor details.

I (*a*) fol. 1*b*. Illuminated title-piece to the first subdivision of the work.

1 fol. 3*b*. Kaiūmarṣ, the first of the Persian kings.

2 fol. 9*b*. Ḍaḥḥāk, the tyrant of Babylon and Arabia, had foreseen Farīdūn, his vanquisher, in a dream, and learns from his priests the import of the vision.

3 fol. 15*a*. Farīdūn is about to slay the serpent-shouldered Ḍaḥḥāk, but decides to bind him for thousands of years.

4 fol. 22*a*. Īraj, the son of Farīdūn, is slain by his brothers Salm and Tūr.

5 fol. 32*a*. The fabulous bird Sīmurgh restores the youthful Zāl to his father Sām, who had abandoned him when an infant on account of his having been born with white hair.

6 fol. 49*a*. The marriage of Zāl and Rūdābah. (It may be observed that in cutting the margin of this page a

part of a man's figure has been trimmed off, leaving the nuptial torch, his hand, and a portion of the turban.)

7 fol. 61*b*. Naudhar, captured by Afrāsiāb, is put to death.

8 fol. 67*b*. Rustam in combat with Afrāsiāb seizes him by the girdle and lifts him from the saddle; Afrāsiāb is saved by the girdle s breaking.

9 fol. 77*b*. Rustam killing the Dīv-i Safīd, or White Demon.

10 fol. 88*b*. Kai Kā'ūs (a pioneer in aviation!) attempts to fly to heaven by fastening young eagles to his throne. (The eagles endeavored to reach the haunches of mutton stuck on the points of four spears at the corners of the throne and thus raised it to the sky; but the eagles, before long, became exhausted, and then Kai Kā'ūs fell from aloft, but escaped death.)

11 fol. 103*b*. Rustam in combat kills Suhrāb, his son.

12 fol. 113*b*. Siāwush passes through the fire-ordeal to prove his innocence of the calumnious charge that he was in love with his stepmother.

13 fol. 125*a*. Siāwush displaying his skill in polo before Afrāsiāb.

14 fol. 139*b*. Siāwush slain at the hand of Gurwī Zirah.

15 fol. 154*b*. Pīrān taken and bound by Gīv.

II (*b*) fol. 161*b*. Illuminated title-piece to the second subdivision of the work, or 'Book of Kai Khusrau.'

16 fol. 162*b*. Rustam and his father Zāl come to congratulate Kai Khusrau on being made King.

17 fol. 177*b*. Pīrān's night attack upon the Īrānians.

18 fol. 201*a*. Ashkābūs slain by Rustam.

19 fol. 213*a*. Rustam catches with his lasso the Khāqān, or Ruler of China, and pulls him down from his white elephant.

20 fol. 222*b*. Rustam wrestling with Pūlādwand of Tūrān. (In the picture is to be noticed a Muḥammadan flag with the words, 'O God, O Muḥammad!')

21 fol. 232*a*. Bīzhan is brought before Afrāsiāb by Garsīwaz, the latter's brother, and is threatened with death for having entered the palace of Manīzhah, the daughter of Afrāsiāb.

22 fol. 243*b*. Rustam taking Bīzhan out of the pit where he had been placed by Afrāsiāb.

23 fol. 258*a*. Rustam in combat with his unrecognized grandson Barzū, the son of Suhrāb, on horseback.

24 fol. 277*a*. The mother of Barzū explains that the man with whom Rustam is fighting is the son of Suhrāb, and therefore Rustam's own grandson.

25 fol. 294*b*. Rustam wrestling with Pīlsam.

26 fol. 313*a*. Hūmān slain in battle by Bīzhan.

27 fol. 333*b*. Kai Khusrau comes to Gūdarz and sees those who have been slain.

28 fol. 345*a*. Shīdah slain by Kai Khusrau.

29 fol. 369*b*. Afrāsiāb and Garsīwaz put to death by Kai Khusrau.

30 fol. 389*a*. Gushtāsp killing a dragon.

31 fol. 417*a*. Asfandiār kills a Sīmurgh bird which attacks his chariot.

32 fol. 442*a*. Rustam shoots Asfandiār in the eyes with an arrow, as the Sīmurgh had bidden him.

III (*c*) fol. 446*b*. Illuminated title-piece to the third subdivision of the work, or 'Book of Bahman.'

33 fol. 462*a*. Bahman the guest of Lūlū.

34 fol. 483*a*. Rustam, though dying, transfixes by an arrow through the plane tree his half-brother Shaghād, who had treacherously caused his death.

35 fol. 500*a*. Farāmarz fights with Bahman and is slain.

36 fol. 518*a*. Bahman in the mausoleum of Gushtāsp. (There is a verse on the sarcophagus to the effect that those who have departed from this life have passed through dust to paradise.)

37 fol. 555*a*. Bahman swallowed by a dragon.

IV (*d*) fol. 556*b*. Illuminated title-piece to the fourth subdivision of the work, or 'Book of Alexander.'

38 fol. 567*a*. Alexander lamenting the death of Darius III, who has been assassinated by two of his own treacherous vizirs.

39 fol. 588*a*. Alexander and Khiḍr, the Sage of Eternal Youth, at the Fountain of Life.

40 fol. 595*a*. Death of Alexander.

2

Firdausī: Shāh-nāmah, or 'Book of Kings,' the great epic poem of Persia, complete in a manuscript dated 1602 A.D., with richly ornate borders and illuminated by seventy-two small miniatures. It carries the narrative to the end, including the circumstances following the death of Yazdagard, and gives also Firdausī's Epilogue. Of the Preface only the last page containing the list of kings from Farīdūn to Yazdagard III has been preserved; the preceding ten folios are missing. The manuscript is contemporary with the close of the reign of the Mughal Emperor Akbar the Great, and in style it belongs to the group of Indian manuscripts of the Mughal period.

Size. — 13¾ × 8½ in. (35.5 × 21.5 cm.). Height and width of written page, respectively, 8 × 4½ in. (20.3 × 11.5 cm.). Folios 581. There are errors in the Persian numbering that is inserted between the lower left-hand columns. Two leaves are lost between fol. 2 and 3, and the first ten folios of the Preface are missing. The number of couplets in the manuscript is about 57,000.

Binding. — Heavy Oriental leather binding of a golden brown color, richly embossed in gilt on the outside, with a mahogany red leather finish on the inside and ornate tooling in various colors. The pressed leather work on both the inside and outside of the covers, with medallions and paneled borders, is very fine. The codex has been bound a second time and subjected to a very slight trimming.

Writing and Paper. — Written in a handsome Nasta'līq character, rather small in size, 25 lines to a page in four gold-ruled columns with rubric section-headings. The paper is of the finest quality and each written page is inset. The decorative margins which form the borders are of a salmon-pink color and are embellished in highly ornate fashion, with varied designs of animals, birds, and flowers, outlined in gold. No two pages are exactly alike, and the grouping as a whole is different in each of the four subdivisions of the codex. The three fly-leaves at the front and the back of the codex are of a different quality from the body of the work, and are of a later date, though one in each case is rather old.

Date and Scribe. — The date is in the colophon on fol. 581*a* as 'Saturday, the first day of Muḥarram, 1011 A.H. [= June 21, 1602 A.D.].' The copyist's name is likewise given in this colophon as Kamāl ad-Dīn bin Ibrāhīm. On fol. 186*a*, in a small colophon at the end of the first subdivision is given a date, 'the seventeenth of the month Shawwāl,' but no year is added.

Memorandums. — At the top of the first older fly-leaf is a memorandum in Persian stating that the work 'contains seventy-five [*sic*] illustrations.' Below this is another Persian entry in the same hand stating that 'Farhād, the son of the Crown Prince, duly purchased this on the 25th of Rabī' aṣ-Ṣānī, 1296 A.H. [= April 18, 1879 A.D.].' A third memorandum in Persian in still the same cursive hand adds a comment on the miniatures as follows: 'The painting in this book is Chinese work; in that territory the beard is very scanty, and for that reason the artist has everywhere drawn Rustam without a beard; it is absurd to paint Rustam as beardless.' It may be noted, however, that on fol. 349*a* and 354*b*, Rustam has a beard.

Subject and Arrangement. — The great epic poem of Persia in nearly sixty thousand couplets, including Firdausī's Epilogue (cf. tr. Mohl 7. 407–409; tr. Pizzi, 8. 472–474) and the end of the 'Older Preface,' the portion devoted to a list of the kings from Farīdūn to Yazdagard III, the preceding ten folios that probably contained the 'Bāisunghar Preface' being missing. In this copy four subdivisions are marked, each introduced by an ʻunwān, or illuminated head-piece. The beginnings of these different parts are as follows: a (fol. 1a). Close of a Preface. — I (fol. 1b–186a). The opening of the poem. — II (fol. 186b–309a). The story of Bīzhan and Manīzhah. — III (fol. 309b–457a). The Reign of Gushtāsp. — IV (fol. 457b–581a). King Anūshīrwān the Just.

Illuminations and Illustrations. — In addition to the ornate borders described above and the illuminated page-headings as introductions to the four separate subdivisions made in the manuscript, there are seventy-two small miniatures, which are called 'Chinese work' in the Persian memorandum on the first older fly-leaf, as noted above. In style, however, these paintings seem to show a strong Indian influence and are perhaps the work of a Mongolian or Turkistān artist who was in Northern India, though he knew Persia as well. They all seem to be the work of a single brush, and are delicate in form and in execution. Each miniature occupies about one-third of the page, and the shape is not square, but in three panels, usually with the middle section considerably larger than the side sections. On fol. 78b and 418a, near the miniatures, the text is embellished by setting some of the verses in ornamental squares, a feature more common in other manuscripts. Somewhat unusual in illustrating the Shāh-nāmah is the introduction, at the close of each of the first three subdivisions of the work, of a painting representing a conventional scene between two lovers. Particularly noteworthy are the beautiful designs in gilt on the salmon-pink margins of each page, because they show the greatest variety in conception, no two being exactly alike. Up to fol. 447a the outline of the figures is given sharpness by a black ink pen-line.

I (*a*) fol. 1*a*. Small illuminated bird design below the list of the Persian kings at the end of the Preface.

(*b*) fol. 2*a*. Illuminated title-piece to the Shāh-nāmah.

1 fol. 2*a*. King Kaiūmarṣ, the first of the line of Persian kings.

2 fol. 3*b*. Jamshīd, the ruler of the Golden Age, sitting on his throne. (In the upper part of the picture, the *dīvs*, 'demons,' *murgh*, 'birds,' and *parīs*, 'fairies,' are shown as his servitors.)

3 fol. 6*a*. Ḍaḥḥāk, the tyrant of Babylon and Arabia, from whose shoulders serpents grew, and whose cruel sway over Persia lasted a thousand years.

4 fol. 27*a*. Īraj, the son of Farīdūn, slain by his own brothers Salm and Tūr.

5 fol. 35*a*. King Minūchihr on his throne.

6 fol. 37*a*. Zāl is restored by the fabulous bird Sīmurgh, to his father, Sām, who had abandoned him on account of the child's having been born with white hair.

7 fol. 42*a*. Zāl woos the beautiful Rūdābah.

8 fol. 52*a*. The birth of the hero Rustam through an incision made in his mother's side. The fabulous bird Sīmurgh appears with timely help. (The Caesarian operation is illustrated in the picture.)

9 fol. 64*a*. In a battle between the Īrānians and Tūrānians, in the time of Kai Qubād, the heroic Rustam, though still a mere youth, lifts Afrāsiāb, the leader of Tūrān, from his saddle by the girdle; but the foeman escapes, as the belt breaks.

10 fol. 79*a*. Kai Kā'ūs attempts to fly to heaven by fastening young eagles to his throne. The eagles try to reach the haunches of meat which he caused to be fastened above on spear-points, and thus they raise the throne to the sky; but King Kā'ūs (the first aviator) comes to grief.

11 fol. 93*a*. Rustam in combat kills Suhrāb, being unaware that he was slaying his own son.

12 fol. 107*a*. Siāwush sends a message to Afrāsiāb of Tūrān by Sangah of Shāvarān.

13 fol. 120*b*. Gurwī Zirah puts to death Siāwush, whom he has captured, and causes the blood to be caught in a basin to send to King Kā'ūs of Īrān.

14 fol. 135*b*. Kai Khusrau sitting in state.

15 fol. 142*b*. Farūd in battle slays Zarāsp, the son of Ṭūs.

16 fol. 150*a*. Battle between Gūdarz and his followers and Pīrān of Tūrān.

17 fol. 167*a*. Rustam in battle with Ashkābūs.

18 fol. 176*a*. The Ruler of China taken prisoner by Rustam with his lasso.

19 fol. 185*a*. The demon Akwān Dīv throws Rustam into the sea.

20 fol. 186*a*. Conventional scene between lovers at the close of the first subdivision of the work. (See comment above.)

II (*c*) fol. 186*b*. Illuminated title-piece to the second subdivision of the work, beginning with the Story of Bīzhan and Manīzhah.

21 fol. 198*b*. Rustam rescues Bīzhan from the well.

22 fol. 200*a*. Rustam in battle with Afrāsiāb of Tūrān.

23 fol. 234*b*. Killing of Pīlsam by Rustam.

24 fol. 237*b*. Battle between Barzū, the grandson of Rustam, and Afrāsiāb of Tūrān.

25 fol. 248*a*. Hūmān slain by Bīzhan.

26 fol. 261*a*. The Tūrānian leader Pīrān killed by Gūdarz in combat.

27 fol. 272*b*. King Khusrau of Īrān slays Shīdah of Tūrān in combat.

28 fol. 274*a*. Battle between Kai Khusrau and Afrāsiāb.

29 fol. 290*a*. Khusrau kills Garsīwaz and likewise Afrāsiāb as the latter comes out of the water.

30 fol. 309*a*. Conventional scene of two lovers at the close of the second subdivision of the work. (See remark above.)

III (*d*) fol. 309*b*. Illuminated title-piece to the third subdivision of the work, beginning with the Reign of Gushtāsp.

31 fol. 309*b*. King Gushtāsp (the patron of Zoroaster) on his throne.

32 fol. 319*b*. Gushtāsp throws his son Asfandiār into prison.

33 fol. 326*b*. Asfandiār kills a wolf on the first stage of his seven adventures.

34 fol. 326*b*. Asfandiār kills a lion and lioness on the second stage of his seven adventures.

35 fol. 327*a*. Asfandiār kills a dragon on the third stage of his seven adventures.

36 fol. 328*a*. Asfandiār kills a sorceress on the fourth stage.

37 fol. 328*b*. Asfandiār kills the Sīmurgh on the fifth stage.

38 fol. 330*b*. Asfandiār kills Gurgsar of Tūrān on the seventh stage. [The sixth stage is not illustrated.]

39 fol. 349*a*. Rustam slays Asfandiār with a two-pronged arrow shot into his eyes.

40 fol. 351*b*. Funeral of Asfandiār.

41 fol. 354*a*. Rustam, though near death, transfixes his treacherous half-brother Shaghād through a tree behind which he had taken refuge.

42 fol. 307*a*. Farāmarz executed by Bahman.

43 fol. 366*a*. Alexander over the corpse of Dārā (Darius III), who has been slain by his own faithless vizirs.

44 fol. 367*a*. Alexander on the throne of Persia.

45 fol. 373*a*. Battle between Alexander and Poros of India.

46 fol. 381*b*. Khiḍr, the Sage of Eternal Youth, at the Fountain of Life — (a part of the legend of Alexander).

47 fol. 384*b*. Alexander returning from China.

48 fol. 389*a*. Story of Ardawān and Ardashīr.

49 fol. 391*b*. Ardawān put to death by Ardashīr.

50 fol. 395*b*. Ardashīr Bābagān on the throne.

51 fol. 406*a*. Shāpūr Dhu'l-Aktāf II, the Sāsānian king (309–379 A.D.).

52 fol. 414*b*. Yazdagard on his throne.

53 fol. 416*b*. Bahrām Gūr hunting in company with his mistress, Fitnah, 'Mischief,' called also Āzādah, 'Noble-born' — the familiar story of how he transfixed the gazelle's hoof to its ear by an arrow, as a proof of his skill in archery.

54 fol. 418*b*. Yazdagard killed by the kick of a horse that came up from the lake in the region of Nīshāpūr.

55 fol. 420*a*. Bahrām Gūr congratulated on ascending the throne.

56 fol. 421*b*. Bahrām Gūr as king.

57 fol. 425*b*. Story of Bahrām Gūr and the chief of the village, who mastered a lion.

58 fol. 431*a*. Story of Bahrām Gūr and the jeweler whose daughter he took as spouse.

59 fol. 444*b*. Bahrām Gūr kills a dragon.

60 fol. 456*b*. Mazdak the Heretic, executed by Anūshīrwān.

61 fol. 457*a*. Conventional scene of lovers at the close of the third subdivision of the work. (See comment above.)

IV (*e*) fol. 457*b*. Illuminated title-piece to the fourth subdivision of the work, beginning with the Reign of Anūshīrwān.

62 fol. 457*b*. Anūshīrwān the Just on the throne.

63 fol. 485*a*. The origin of the game of chess.

64 fol. 490*b*. Battle between Gīv and Talkhand; the latter is slain on the back of his elephant.

65 fol. 512*a*. Battle between Bahrām Chūbīn and Sāwah-Shāh, and death of the latter.

66 fol. 530*b*. Bahrām Chūbīn sits on the throne at Ctesiphon.

67 fol. 548*b*. Death of Bahrām Chūbīn by the hand of Qālūn.

68 fol. 556*b*. Khusrau, out hunting, meets Shīrīn.

69 fol. 559*a*. King Khusrau and the minstrel Bārbad, who, unknown to the King, sang hidden between two cypress branches and thus became court bard.

70 fol. 568*b*. Khusrau Parwīz slain by Mihr Hurmazd.

71 fol. 572*a*. Yazdagard III on the throne.

72 fol. 578*b*. Yazdagard assassinated.

3

Firdausī: Shāh-nāmah. — An illuminated manuscript of the Shāh-nāmah belonging to the beginning of the seventeenth century (being dated 1605–1608 A.D.). It has an introduction (the so-called 'Older Preface') and carries the epic narrative to the end, including the death of Yazdagard III. It inserts Firdausī's lament over the death of his own son in place of the ordinary Epilogue. This handsome manuscript is adorned by eighty-five large miniatures.

Size. — 14¾ × 9¾ in. (37.4 × 25.0 cm.). Width of written page 5⅛ in. (13.0 cm.) with large margins, height 11¾ in. (29.6 cm.). Folios 571. One folio is missing between fol. 429 and 430; and there is a slight misbinding between folios 225–232, where the proper order would be fol. 225, 231, 227, 228, 229, 230, 226, 232. The number of distichs is somewhat under 45,000.

Binding. — Old lacquer covers with floral designs, including a large bunch of flowers on an orange background, and with delicate marginal gold decorations. The inside leather is of a dull green. The stitched head-binding is in the Shīrāzī style; and small silk tabs are attached to the margin of the folios that contain illustrations.

Writing and Paper. — Handsome Nasta'līq hand, 21 lines to the page in four columns with marginal rulings of gold, blue, red, and green. The paper is of a rich cream tint and varies considerably as to weight and quality in different parts of the codex.

Date and Scribe. — The date of the manuscript is found in two different places (fol. 309*a* and fol. 571*a*) and shows that the copying of the codex occupied a period of more than two years, possibly four. On fol. 309*a*, the colophon says: 'Finished the first volume, by the help of God, in the year 1014 A.H. [= 1605 A.D.].' On the last folio (fol. 571*a*), in a longer colophon, the date of completion is given as 1016 A.H. = 1608 A.D., together with the name of the scribe, and reads as follows: 'The book was finished by the help of God, the Lord of Mercy and Grace, on the twelfth day of the month of Sha'bān in the year 1016 A.H. [= Dec. 2, 1608 A.D.]; written by the poor and sinful servant and solicitor of pardon from God, Master Muḥammad, the son of Mullā Mīr, al-Ḥusainī (may God forgive him, and forgive the artist and whosoever does any work with it!). The request I ask from my friends is a prayer that God may accept it as a means for my salvation.'[1]

Memorandums. — On each side of the last folio is an impression of a large square seal, but in it only the name Muḥammad can be deciphered, the rest being indistinct or obliterated. On the middle of the last page is a Persian jotting, 'He is God the Most High.' Below it is a nearly erased memorandum of no importance, but it is possible to make out a few words, 'eighth of Jumādī II, [*year illegible*], Isfahān.'

Subject and Arrangement. — The great epic of Firdausī complete with an introduction on the life and work of the poet. The introduction (fol. 1*b*–7*a*) corresponds to the so-called 'Older Preface' and includes Firdausī's Satire against Maḥmūd (fol. 5*a*–5*b*). Folios 7*b* and 8*a* are blank, the epic itself beginning on fol. 8*b*. At the end of the manuscript, before the colophon, there is given Firdausī's lament over the death of his son, instead of the usual Epilogue. It may be noted

[1] This Master Muḥammad, son of Mullā Mīr, of the sect of Ḥusain, is possibly the same as Muḥammad Ḥusain, from Kashmīr, a famous calligraphist at the court of Akbar the Great; he is spoken of in the royal chronicles as 'the equal of Mullā Mīr 'Alī' and was generally known by the complimentary title of *Zarīn Qalam*, or 'Golden Pen.' (See also Sachau and Ethé, *Cat. Pers. Mss.*, col. 634, no. 963; and Browne, *Cat. Pers. Mss. Lib. Cambridge*, p. 331, no. 235.) From the date given at the end of the first subdivision of the manuscript (see above), he must have begun the copying some time before the death of Akbar, which occurred on Oct. 13, 1605; and he completed it when Jahāngīr had been three years on the throne. For a reference to him as celebrated among the masters of Nasta'līq handwriting, see Abu'l Faḍl, *Ā'in-i Akbarī, or Institutes of Akbar*, tr. F. Gladwin, I. 112, London, 1800.

that the manuscript is divided into two parts by an illuminated caption at fol. 310*b*, beginning with the reign of Luhrāsp.

Illuminations and Illustrations. — The manuscript is illuminated by handsomely adorned title-pages and decorative headbands, and is richly provided with miniatures, which number no less than eighty-five and are nearly full-page. The copyist, as noted above, speaks of the 'artist,' but does not mention his name. In style these miniatures, with the exception of two (38 and 39), as noted below, seem to be the work of a single hand throughout and show a touch of Chinese influence in the manner of conception and execution. In a number of miniatures the background or side decoration is carried well out into the margin — a feature that is found in other manuscripts as well. The oft-repeated use of the two long-tailed magpies in the miniature scenes gives an impression almost like the artist's signature in modern etchings. Especial attention must be given, by art students, to the fact that the two remarkable miniatures on fol. 175*a* and 175*b*, which are full of spirit, are certainly by another artist than the one who executed the rest of the work. Internal evidence, noted below, shows that there is a lacuna following these two special miniatures.

I (*a*) fol. 1*b*. Illuminated title-pages to the Preface.

(*b*) fol. 8*b*. Illuminated full-page opening of the *Shāh-nāmah*.

(*c*) fol. 9*a*. Illuminated full-page containing the opening verses.

1 fol. 12*a*. Kaiūmarş, the first king, tasting of the products of the earth.

2 fol. 14*a*. Tahmūraş combats the Dīvs, or Demons.

3 fol. 22*a*. Farīdūn is about to slay the serpent-shouldered Ḍaḥḥāk, but decides to bind him as a prisoner for thousands of years.

4 fol. 23*b*. Farīdūn enthroned.

5 fol. 33*b*. War between Minūchihr and Tūr; death of Tūr.
6 fol. 36*b*. Enthronement of Minūchihr.
7 fol. 39*a*. Meeting between Minūchihr and Sām; Sām out of respect kisses the foot of Minūchihr.
8 fol. 53*a*. Zāl and Rūdābah meet when they are out riding.
9 fol. 60*a*. Kai Qubād, before his combat with Bārmān, gives instructions about his own burial.
10 fol. 62*a*. Zāl killing Khusrawān in single combat with his mace.
11 fol. 67*a*. Battle of Rustam of Īrān and Afrāsiāb of Tūrān.
12 fol. 73*a*. Rustam's horse Rakhsh kills a lion and saves his master.
13 fol. 74*b*. Rustam killing the dragon.
14 fol. 75*a*. Rustam and the Enchantress, whom he afterwards slays.
15 fol. 76*a*. Rustam nooses Ūlād with his lasso.
16 fol. 77*a*. Rustam and the Dīv Arzhang in combat.
17 fol. 78*a*. Rustam kills the White Dīv in his cavern and releases Kā'ūs and the Īrānians from the prison of the Dīv.
18 fol. 81*a*. Battle of Kai Kā'ūs with the king of Māzandarān.
19 fol. 83*b*. War between Kā'ūs and Hāmāvarān, the king of Barbaristān, or Yaman.
20 fol. 86*b*. The king of Hāmāvarān overpowered by Rustam.
21 fol. 91*a*. Rustam captures Afrāsiāb of Tūrān in battle.
22 fol. 92*b*. Tahmīnah, the daughter of the king of Samangān, visits Rustam and conceives by him a son, Suhrāb.
23 fol. 95*a*. Suhrāb discovers that his combatant is a woman in disguise, the daughter of Guzhdahm, an Īrānian warrior.
24 fol. 101*a*. Combat of Suhrāb and Rustam.
25 fol. 104*a*. Death of Suhrāb by the hand of his father Rustam.
26 fol. 105*a*. The body of Suhrāb is carried to Zābulistān; Rustam accompanies it with lamentation.
27 fol. 109*a*. Feasting and merrymaking at the birth of Siāwush.
28 fol. 114*a*. Siāwush passes through the fire-ordeal to prove his innocence of the accusation of his stepmother, Sūdābah.

29 fol. 124*a*. Siāwush visits Afrāsiāb of Tūrān.

30 fol. 125*b*. Siāwush exhibits to Afrāsiāb and the Turks his skill in polo.

31 fol. 126*b*. Siāwush shows his skill in the chase with Afrāsiāb and arouses the envy of the Turks.

32 fol. 138*a*. Gurwī Zirah cuts off the head of Siāwush and lets the blood flow into a basin.

33 fol. 143*b*. The king of Sanjāb (or Sipanjāb) killed by the hand of Farāmarz, the son of Rustam.

34 fol. 146*a*. A combat between Rustam and Afrāsiāb.

35 fol. 161*a*. Rustam, Zāl, and Sām come to see Kai Khusrau.

36 fol. 164*a*. Kai Khusrau mounted on an elephant reviews the army, accompanied by his warriors, Farīburz and Gūdarz.

37 fol. 173*b*. Battle between the Īrānians and Tūrānians led respectively by Bīzhan and Tazhau.

38 fol. 175*a*. Pīrān's night attack upon the Īrānians. (This picture and its mate on the following page differ in style of art from the other miniatures in the manuscript, as observed above.)

39 fol. 175*b*. Combat the next day. (See preceding note and observe that fol. 174*b* is incomplete, and a lacuna follows fol. 175*b*, equivalent to the text in the Vullers-Landauer edition, vol. 2, p. 840, l. 1201, as far as p. 857, l. 1498.)

40 fol. 187*a*. The marriage of Farīburz and Farangīs, the mother of Kai Khusrau.

41 fol. 195*a*. Rustam kills Ashkābūs, the leader of the Tūrānians.

42 fol. 205*b*. Rustam with his noose lassoes Gahār of Gahān, the Khāqān of China, and pulls him down from his white elephant.

43 fol. 213*b*. Rustam wrestling with Pūlādwand of Gurān.

44 fol. 216*a*. Rustam carried off in his sleep by the demon Akwān Dīv, who throws him into the sea.

45 fol. 229*b*. Kai Khusrau receives Rustam.

46 fol. 235*b*. Rustam taking Bīzhan out of the well where he was placed by Afrāsiāb.

47 fol. 249*a*. Hūmān meets death at the hand of Bīzhan.

48 fol. 261*a*. Farīburz in combat with Kulbād, a Tūrānian hero.

49 fol. 251*b*. Gīv captures Gurwī.

50 fol. 268*b*. Kai Khusrau destroys the army of the Tūrānians and kills the hero Gurwī.

51 fol. 279*a*. Shīdah, the son of Afrāsiāb, is put to death by Kai Khusrau.

52 fol. 288*a*. Kai Khusrau in the harem of Afrāsiāb gives quarter to the ladies.

53 fol. 295*a*. Kai Khusrau crosses the sea of Zirih.

54 fol. 300*b*. Afrāsiāb slain by the sword of Kai Khusrau.

II (*d*) fol. 310*b*. Illuminated title-piece introducing the second part of *Shāh-nāmah*.

55 fol. 316*a*. Gushtāsp slays a wolf.

56 fol. 320*a*. Gushtāsp fights with Iliās and slays him.

57 fol. 333*b*. Gushtāsp imprisons his own son, Asfandiār.

58 fol. 344*a*. The first stage — Asfandiār killing two wolves.

59 fol. 344*b*. The second stage — Asfandiār killing two lions.

60 fol. 345*b*. The third stage — Asfandiār killing a dragon.

61 fol. 346*b*. The fourth stage — Asfandiār killing a witch.

62 fol. 347*b*. The fifth stage — Asfandiār killing the Sīmurgh.

63 fol. 374*b*. Rustam transfixes Shaghād through the plane tree by his arrow. (Shaghād was the son of Zāl by a slave wife, and was consequently a half-brother of Rustam.)

64 fol. 378*a*. Bīshūtan, the Minister of Bahman (Ardashīr), son of Asfandiār, admonishes his lord Bahman, after the latter had impaled Farāmarz in revenge for the death of Shaghād, to stop the pillaging of the country. Bahman repents of his act.

65 fol. 388*a*. Alexander discovers that Dārā (Darius III) has been assassinated by two of his own treacherous vizirs.

66 fol. 391*b*. Rūshanak, the daughter of Darius, in the presence of Alexander.

67 fol. 397*a*. Alexander at the gate of the Ka'ba in Mecca.

68 fol. 418*a*. Ardashīr recognizes Ormazd, the son of Shāpūr I, as the boy is playing polo.

69 fol. 425*a*. Crowning of Shāpūr II while yet a small boy.

70 fol. 429*a*. Shāpūr attacks by night the camp of the Romans and takes captive the Roman emperor.

71 fol. 432*b*. Bahrām Gūr shows his skill in archery by transfixing the hoof of the deer to its ear. His mistress Āzādah (elsewhere called Fitnah, 'Mischief') is playing on the harp. (The episode has already been alluded to.)

72 fol. 436*b*. Bahrām Gūr killing lions.

73 fol. 448*a*. Bahrām wrestles with a champion in the court of Shangil, king of India, and shows his prowess.

74 fol. 450*b*. Bahrām marries Sapīnūd, the daughter of Shangil.

75 fol. 460*b*. The court of Anūshīrwān the Just.

76 fol. 467*a*. Buzurjmihr interpreting the dream of Anūshīrwān.

77 fol. 475*b*. Anūshīrwān marries the daughter of the Khāqān of China.

78 fol. 497*b*. Bahrām Chūbīnah cuts off the head of King Sāwah and sends it to Hurmuzd.

79 fol. 509*a*. Chūbīnah humbled before Khusrau Parwīz.

80 fol. 534*b*. Bahrām Chūbīnah killing a dragon.

81 fol. 551*a*. Khusrau and his attendants.

82 fol. 555*b*. Qubād Shīrū'ī, the son of Khusrau Parwīz, ascends the throne and puts the crown upon his head and is honored by the heroes of Īrān.

83 fol. 561*a*. Rustam slain in a combat with Sa'd, the son of Waqqās, an Arab.

84 fol. 566*b*. A miller, by the order of Mahwī Sūrī, kills King Yazdagard III and throws the body into the water.

85 fol. 569*b*. Bīzhan tortures and kills Mahwī Sūrī in revenge for Yazdagard's murder.

4

Firdausī: Shāh-nāmah. — A handsome, large, and very fully illuminated and illustrated manuscript belonging to the middle of the seventeenth century (being dated 1663–1669 A.D.) and carrying the epic narrative down to the death of Rustam and the events preceding the death of Yazdagard III. It contains Firdausī's Epilogue and is introduced by the two Prefaces described below. The codex has forty-two beautiful miniatures and is part cularly interesting because of the signatures of the different artists attached to most of the paintings. The lacquer covers show much taste.

Size. — $18\frac{1}{2} \times 11\frac{1}{8}$ in. (46.5×28.5 cm.); written surface, $13\frac{3}{8} \times 6\frac{7}{8}$ in. (34.0×17.5 cm.). Folios 460. Total number of couplets about 55,000. There are no folios missing.

Binding. — Persian lacquer covers of about a century ago, when the manuscript appears to have been rebound, if we may judge by the date of the introduction which was added in 1255 A.H. = 1839 A.D. Both covers are tastefully decorated within and without. The outside covers are of a ruby tinge with a rich ornamentation of flower and bird designs. In the center, moreover, of the outside of the front cover there is portrayed one of the Persian kings seated upon his throne with a youth, probably his son, standing by him. On the king's right is seated a warrior, presumably Rustam, if we may judge from his mace and cap, and from the general portraiture of that hero in Shāh-nāmah manuscripts. To the left of the king there is seated a white-bearded hero, but there is nothing to identify him or the monarch himself. The shape of the king's crown and of the swords and shields betrays the more modern style of this binding, and the same is true of the two little scenes in the small panels above and below the centerpiece, one of which shows a bridge and a building, while the other shows two houses. In the center of the outside of the back cover is another picture, apparently by a different artist, representing likewise a royal personage on his throne, attended by a prince, a warrior, and two pages, but there is nothing by which to identify these personages. Above and below are small vignette scenes similar in style to those on the front cover. The inside covers are of olive-green lacquer with ruby medallions and borders, the field in each case being enriched by a graceful design of golden flowers, garlands, and the tips of peacock feathers; the whole finish shows workmanship of the highest order.

The manuscript was received in an old Oriental case of heavy dark leather.

Writing and Paper. — Elegant Nasta'līq hand of a medium size, 31 lines to the page in four columns, with marginal rulings of gold, blue, red, and green. The paper of the codex is of a light cream color and of an unusually fine quality; the screen-marks are very close together. The paper used in the Preface, which has been added, and that of the fly-leaves is of much later date. In rebinding, the margins of the folios have been somewhat trimmed, so that in a number of instances the catchwords have been cropped off; occasionally these are supplied in a later hand.

Date and Scribe. — The date of the manuscript, 1663–1669 A.D., and the name of the copyist, Bin Shams ad-Dīn Shaikh Muḥammad, are both given. A comparison of the different parts of the codex shows that its preparation was the work of over six years. The date at the end of the first subdivision, fol. 238*a*, is given as 'the month of Ṣafar, 1074 A.H. [= Sept. 1663 A.D.]'; and the date at the end of the second, or last subdivision, fol. 460*a*, is recorded as 'the last day of Shawwāl, 1079 A.H. [= April 2, 1669 A.D.]'; the entire sentence which contains this latter date and the scribe's name reads as follows: 'The book of Shāh-nāmah was finished by the help of God the Most High and under His kind guidance, on the last day of Shawwāl, the month of merit and success, the year of the Hijrat of the Prophet one thousand and seventy and nine, 1079 [*sic*] A.H. [= April 2, 1669 A.D.]; it was written by the most humble servant Bin Shams ad-Dīn Shaikh Muḥammad; may God forgive him on this account [*i.e.* through the merit accrued by copying it].'

Memorandums. — There are several seals of different owners into whose possession the manuscript came; three of these, for example, are impressed upon the back of the last folio (460*b*). The largest of these three seals on fol. 460*b* is that to the left of the page, bearing the inscription, 'Shāh Jahān sanah aḥad Ṭayyib Khān fidawī.' [1] Above the seal there is the following memorandum in Persian: 'Shāh-nāmah, copied by Shams ad-Dīn Muḥammad; the paintings in it are the work of Āqā Nūyān and other artists, [*a word cut off*] five pictures; price one hundred and ten tūmāns; it was presented in the month of Shawwāl, year . . . [*the figures cut off in rebinding*].'

The seal next in size, towards the right of the page, is indistinct in regard to the name, which is different, however,

[1] The two words *sanah aḥad*, 'first (regnal) year,' might possibly suggest that this large seal may have been a signet connected with the Mughal Emperor, Shāh Jahān, who ruled over India 1628–1658 and died in 1666 — or three years before this manuscript was finally completed — but if so, the seal would have to be explained as having been affixed by one of Shāh Jahān's officials when the copy came into the royal library after his death. It might be possible to venture a conjecture that this Ṭayyib Khān was the same as Shāh Ṭayyib, a prince who was also a poet, belonging to this period, as mentioned by Pertsch, *Verzeichniss der Handschriften der kgl. Bibl. zu Berlin, Persische Handschriften*, p. 606, no. 39, Berlin, 1888.

from the preceding and appears to be 'Muḥammad bin . . . Ṭayyib Khān,' and above it in the body of the seal is the date 1128 A.H. = 1715 A.D.; furthermore, above it is written in Persian: 'Illustrated Shāh-nāmah, the work of Āqā Nūyān and other artists; it was presented on the tenth of the month of Rajab, year . . . [*the figures are illegible*].'

Between these two is a small seal, the signet of 'Muḥammad Hāshim bin Ḥusain al-Ḥusainī.' Above it is a Persian jotting: 'Shāh-nāmah, which was bought for three hundred and twenty tūmāns in 1251 A.H. [= 1835 A.D.].'

Near the top of fol. 9*a* is a more recent seal, the official signet of the Amīr Niẓām (his personal name being Ḥasan 'Alī), who was Governor of Ādharbaijān in 1894 and for several years afterwards. An accompanying Persian memorandum in five lines of large script by this high dignitary reads as follows: 'In the period of my administration in Ādharbaijān, while I was residing at Tabrīz, the seat of government, I bought this book, the Shāh-nāmah, from the honorable and august Āqā Nūr Muḥammad Ḥusain, who is one of the true-born princes [of the house of 'Alī] and who is one of the greatest merchants of Tabrīz . . . for three hundred tūmāns in the month of Rabī' aṣ-Ṣānī 1312 A.H. [= October, 1894 A.D.] — [*signed*] God's servant Ḥasan 'Alī.'

On the upper margin of fol. 48*a* there is a small part of a seal-impression, but it is not legible.

Throughout the course of the manuscript there are numerous marginal jottings, some of which are of special value because they relate to the miniatures, as will be described below; others are merely ordinary memorandums, like the supplying of a verse or verses omitted in the text. It will be noticed, for example, that in the upper left-hand corner of folios 223*a*, 230*a*, and 242*a* there is a note in Persian — 'something must be written' — referring probably to some omission in the text. Some one began to number the folios in the lower left-hand corner in Persian figures as far as fol. 47*b*, but this was carried no farther; and up to 47*b* the sections headed by gold bands were numbered sometimes in the margin and sometimes between the columns, but not systematically, and this also was abandoned. In some instances where the catchwords have been clipped in rebinding, they are supplied in a small hand between the gold rulings. Figures in a minuscule hand are added beneath the miniatures so as to number them, but two of them were accidentally overlooked in numbering. For the other jottings as to the miniatures see below.

Subject and Arrangement. — The great epic of Persia, practically complete, and preceded by an introduction containing 'the Bāisunghar Preface' and 'the Older Preface' (cf. Rieu, *Cat. Pers. Mss. in British Museum*, 2. 534). This particular introduction was copied and added two centuries after the manuscript was prepared, as is shown by the date given at its close as 1255 A.H. = 1839 A.D.; it occupies six and a half folios.

The first part of the introduction (fol. 1*b*–3*a*) contains a list of the early kings of Īrān in the order of their dynasties, Pīshdādian, Kaiānian, Ashkānian, and Sāsānian, together with tables of their reigns and other data, such as their titles, characteristics, capitals, or cities founded, and the like. One column in the table of the Kaiānian rulers, on fol. 2*a*, gives a list of the names of the prophets contemporary with their reigns. The paragraph that follows this table is devoted to a summary of the interregnum of Alexander the Great. The so-called 'Bāisunghar Preface' begins near the top of fol. 3*a* with a doxology and with the special line that is recorded in the second instance by Rieu, 2. 536 (Ms. 27. 302) as follows:—

سپا س مر خدایرا که خداوند دو جهان است

An account is given of Firdausī's life and of the circumstances that led him to undertake the composition of the Shāh-nāmah. Firdausī's celebrated Satire on Sultān Maḥmūd occupies the larger part of fol. 4*a*–4*b* and comprises 60 couplets. After this comes the notice of the degradation of the Vizir Maimandī.

The so-called 'Older Preface' begins four lines from the bottom of fol. 4*b*, with the line

سپاس آفرین خدای را که این جهان وآن جهان آفرید

It contains a briefer account of Firdausī's life and of the great epic and is followed (5*a*) by a list of the Kings of Persia, with the duration of their reigns. After this comes a vocabulary of old or obsolete Persian words that occur in the poem (fol. 5*a*–7*b*). As above noted, when this introduction was prefixed to the codex, which was already nearly two centuries old, a colophon, containing the date 1255 A.H. (= 1839 A.D.), was appended. The entire next folio (8*a*–*b*) is blank, and so is the first half of 9*a*, except for the memorandum noted above. The poem begins on fol. 9*b* and continues unbroken, down to the events preceding the death of Yazdagard III. The Epilogue of Firdausī shows some slight variations from the ordinarily received version (compare tr. Mohl, 7. 407–409; tr. Pizzi, 8. 472–474).

The two subdivisions into which this manuscript divides the poem are very unequal. The first subdivision (I) covers fol. 9*b*–238*a*, the next two pages being left blank. The second subdivision (II) begins on fol. 239*b*, with the 'Reign of Luhrāsp,' and carries the epic to the events just preceding the fall of the Sāsānian empire.

Illuminations and Illustrations. — The manuscript is an ornate one; the embellishment of the title-page is particularly rich, and a number of the pages in the vicinity of miniatures are interlined with gold. The captions of the sections throughout are of gold and inscribed with red ink. In a few instances the verses before or after an illustration are written diagonally in square spaces to give a decorative effect.

In regard to its miniatures (forty-two in number) the manuscript is a specially fine example of the general type of Shāh-nāmah illustration, and most of the paintings are signed. It is possible to recognize five different artists, perhaps the finest being 'Alī Naqī, whose signature, in minuscule hand, is attached to three miniatures as follows: on fol. 24*b*, in the space between the columns, it is written as ''Alī Naqī, the son of Shaikh, 1014'; on fol. 100*a*, upon a brick, it appears as ''Alī Naqī, [the son of] Shaikh 'Abbāsī, year 1014,' and again on fol. 102*a*, upon a vase, as ''Alī Naqī, [the son of] Shaikh 'Abbāsī, 1014.' The year 1014 A.H. would be equivalent to 1605 A.D., but possibly we should read 1104 = 1692 A.D., which is found in the repeated memorandum below the signed miniatures of another artist on fol. 170*b*, 244*b*, as well as (erased but legible) on 230*a*, and, with the figures misplaced (1140 for 1104) on fol. 422*a*. Yet the whole matter is very uncertain. 'Alī Naqī's work is particularly fine in its detail, as is shown by the beautiful miniature on fol. 24*b*.

Next in order may be mentioned the miniatures, presumably by Āqā Nūyān, on fol. 73*b*, 110*b*, 151*b*, as his name is mentioned in the Persian memorandum jotted on the last page, as noted above. In each of these three paintings there is found, apparently as an artist's motto, the phrase 'O Lord of Time,' *i.e.* God.

A third artist, but anonymous, appears to have prepared the miniatures on fol. 36*a*, 47*a*, and 58*a*.

Fourth, and quite distinct in style, is the work of Ghulām Parmāk, whose signature is found in the columns below the painting on 43*b*. From Parmāk's brush come also the miniatures on fol. 11, 31, 51, 53, 55, 64, 69, 71, 84, 91. Noticeable is his use of blue coloring and his method of indicating rocks.

Fifth, but most numerous, are the miniatures by Faḍl 'Alī; he styles himself 'the humble Faḍl 'Alī' and regularly signs his pictures. To him are due twenty-two miniatures as follows: fol. 106, 116, 129, 138, 162, 170, 176, 184, 193, 203, 214, 230, 244, 278, 282, 292, 299, 331, 338, 347, 354, 422. Striking in his work is the use of pink, bright orange, and white, and all his figures are large and boldly drawn.

I (*a*) fol. 1*b*. Illuminated title-piece to the Preface.

(*b*) fol. 9*b*. Illuminated title-page to the first subdivision.

1 fol. 11*b*. The condition of things at the time of Kaiūmarṣ, the first king of Persia, when the people used to wear leopard-skins and the hides of animals.

2 fol. 24*b*. Īraj slain by Salm and Tūr, his brothers; their father, Farīdūn, with his courtiers, laments as the head of Īraj is brought before him. This beautiful miniature, so full of expression, is signed ''Alī Naqī, the son of Shaikh, year 1014,' as noted above.

3 fol. 31*b*. Sām seeking Zāl, his son, who is found in the nest of the fabulous bird Sīmurgh with its young.

4 fol. 36*a*. The meeting of Zāl and Rūdābah, with dancing girls and music.

5 fol. 43*b*. Zāl displays his prowess before Minūchihr, in piercing through the trunk of a large tree with his arrow. Signed in the column below the picture, 'Ghulām Parmāk, 1019.'

6 fol. 47*a*. Rustam kills the white elephant.

7 fol. 51*b*. The third battle between Naudhar and Afrāsiāb.

8 fol. 53*b*. Naudhar slain at the hand of Afrāsiāb.

9 fol. 55*a*. The court of Zav, the son of Tahmāsp.

10 fol. 58*a*. Pashang making merry in his court at the moment when his son Afrāsiāb brings the fearful news of Rustam's martial prowess.

11 fol. 64*b*. Rustam killing the white Dīv in the cavern and releasing Ūlād, who had been made a prisoner by the Dīv.

12 fol. 69*b*. Rustam fights with Arzhang, the king of Baristān, and takes him captive.

13 fol. 71*a*. Kai Kā'ūs attempts to fly to heaven by eagles fastened to his throne and shoots at an angel.

14 fol. 73*b*. Pīlsam in battle against the Īrānians. (On the top of the picture are the words 'O Lord of Time,' *i.e.* God. This phrase may be a motto used by the artist Āqā Nūyān, as already remarked.)

15 fol. 84*a*. Rustam kills Suhrāb. (On Suhrāb's arm is shown the amulet which was bound there as a talisman by his mother.)

16 fol. 91*b*. Siāwush going through the fire-ordeal to prove his innocence of the accusation of a guilty love for Sūdābah, his stepmother.

17 fol. 100*a*. Siāwush displays his skill in the chase, and arouses the envy of Afrāsiāb and the Turks. Signed by 'Alī Naqī, 1014.

18 fol. 102*a*. Siāwush marries the daughter of Afrāsiāb. Signed by 'Alī Naqī.

19 fol. 106*a*. Garsīwaz slandering Siāwush before Afrāsiāb. Signed by Faḍl 'Alī.

20 fol. 110*b*. A meeting of Afrāsiāb and Garsīwaz. (Over the picture are the words 'O Lord of Time,' *i. e.* God. See above, fol. 73*b*.)

21 fol. 116*a*. Battle of Pīlsam against the Īrānians, and the death of Pīlsam. Signed by Faḍl 'Alī.

22 fol. 129*b*. Kai Khusrau rides on an elephant as he reviews his army. Signed by Faḍl 'Alī.

23 fol. 138*b*. Battle between the Persians and the Tūrānians.

24 fol. 151*b*. Rustam comes to the help of the Īrānians against

the Tūrānians. (Again the words 'O Lord of Time.' See above, fol. 73*b*.)

25 fol. 162*a*. Rustam before Kai Khusrau after his capture of the Khāqān of China. Signed at top and bottom by Faḍl 'Alī.

26 fol. 170*b*. Rustam in his sleep carried off by Akwān Dīv, and thrown into the sea. Signed Faḍl 'Alī.

27 fol. 176*b*. Bīzhan imprisoned in a pit is fed by Manīzhah the daughter of Afrāsiāb. Signed Faḍl 'Alī.

28 fol. 184*a*. Bīzhan taken out of the pit by Rustam. Signed Faḍl 'Alī.

29 fol. 193*b*. Hūmān killed by the hand of Bīzhan. Signed Faḍl 'Alī.

30 fol. 203*a*. Gūdarz, the son of Kishwād, fights with Pīrān. Signed Faḍl 'Alī.

31 fol. 214*a*. Kai Khusrau wrestles with Shīdah, and Shīdah is slain by him.

32 fol. 230*a*. Garsīwaz begs Kai Khusrau for mercy, but Kai Khusrau orders him to be cut asunder by the executioner and commands that his brother Afrāsiāb be put to death.—Not signed, but evidently by Faḍl 'Alī.

II (*c*) fol. 239*b*. Illuminated title-page to the second subdivision of the Shāh-nāmah, beginning with the story of Luhrāsp.

33 fol. 244*b*. Gushtāsp killing a dragon. Signed by Faḍl 'Alī.

34 fol. 278*a*. A meeting of Asfandiār and Rustam, after their combat. Signed Faḍl 'Alī.

35 fol. 282*a*. Rustam falls into a spiked pit dug in the hunting-ground by his half-brother Shaghād, the king of Qābūl; but from the pit he transfixes Shaghād through the trunk of a tree, behind which the latter had taken refuge. The signature appears to be missing, but the work is plainly that of Faḍl 'Alī.

36 fol. 292*a*. The death of Darius, and the lament of Alexander. Signed Faḍl 'Alī.

37 fol. 299*a*. Alexander and Khiḍr at the Fountain of Life. (In the picture Alexander rides a white mare accom-

panied by her foal; and Khiḍr is mounted on a mule; to be observed also are the flag-bearer and torch-carrier.)

38 fol. 331*b*. Bahrām Gūr in company with his mistress Fitnah, or Āzādah, who plays on the harp while he transfixes the gazelle's hoof to its ear. Signed Faḍl 'Alī.

39 fol. 338*a*. Bahrām Gūr hunting lions. Not signed, but plainly the work of Faḍl 'Alī.

40 fol. 347*a*. Bahrām Gūr kills a dragon. Signed by Faḍl 'Alī.

41 fol. 354*a*. Bahrām kills another dragon. Signed by Faḍl 'Alī.

42 fol. 422*a*. Combat between Khusrau and Bahrām Chūbīnah. Signed Faḍl 'Alī, 1140 (for 1104; see page 34).

5

Firdausī: Shāh-nāmah. — A large-sized copy of the great epic, belonging possibly to the latter part of the sixteenth century, or to the early seventeenth century, and carrying the heroic story down through Alexander's death. It is handsomely illuminated and is illustrated by twenty-eight miniatures. The embossed covers of the binding are worthy of mention.

Size. — $18\frac{3}{8} \times 12\frac{1}{2}$ in. (46.6×31.6 cm.). Height and width of written page, respectively, $12 \times 7\frac{1}{2}$ in. (30.5×19.3 cm.). Folios 579. The manuscript comprises about 47,500 couplets. One leaf is missing between folios 392 and 393.

Binding. — Strongly bound in olive-brown leather, apparently camel's hide, with flap-cover, and heavily embossed with designs in gold. The covers are the original ones, although the manuscript has been bound a second time, and the workmanship on both covers is alike in all respects.

FARIDUN'S GRIEF AT THE MURDER OF HIS SON, ĪRAJ
Painting by 'Alī Naqī, Ms. No. 4, fol. 21*b* (see page 35)

The outside covers are stamped with a double border that incloses a scene representing trees and shrubs in bloom, with various animals and birds, such as lions, gazelles, deer, foxes, a wild boar, storks, and jackdaws. One of the lions is in the act of killing a wild ram; there is also a brook with a duck and a crane. The marginal borders show panel designs with flowers, birds, and heads of lions impressed in gold.

The inside covers have a highly ornate arabesque design, rich in gold and color, in a setting of dark red leather. The central field is oblong in shape, with gold tooled circular designs upon a background of various colors, green, orange, deep blue, and white. The outer border has paneled work of a similar nature and like colors, except the orange; the inner border is a broad gold band with a running design.

The flap-cover is ornamented inside and out in such a way as to match exactly the respective designs on the exterior and interior binding. On the back of the flap, handsomely inscribed in gold panels, is the following quatrain: —

> 'Blessings upon the soul of Firdausī,
> Who was of sacred and happy origin!
> He was not a mere teacher and we his pupils;
> He was a lord and we his servants!'

In a golden brooch-shaped panel between the two halves of this quatrain is added the invocation, 'The mercy of God (be upon him)!'

Although the manuscript has undergone rebinding, the edges of the pages have not been especially trimmed, except the first folio, which was slightly cut down when it was repaired by a sheet pasted on the back of it, as explained below. The fact that the edges of the folios are gilded — a feature not common in Persian manuscripts — is worth mentioning, and this may well be a later addition. For the purpose of protecting the miniatures, thin paper inserts have been pasted between the folios that contain illustrations, but some of the paintings had previously been slightly marred. For convenience in finding the pictures, tabs with small ribbons attached have been added to the margins of the folios concerned.

Writing and Paper. — Written in a beautiful Nastaʿlīq hand of a rather large size, 21 lines to the page in four columns, with marginal rulings of gold and blue. The paper is of an excellent quality and of a light cream color, with a dull finish, slightly resembling parchment. In composition, the paper is exceptionally even, and might be placed approximately at a sixty-five pound basis. The wire-marks usually show a wide sweeping curve. The two heavy fly-leaves at the front and back are pink on the outer side and are outlined by broad gold rulings. The other two thin fly-leaves front and back, due also to rebinding, are of light-weight European paper. The first folio has been repaired by a sheet pasted on the back. This can be clearly seen by holding the leaf up to the light. It contained the conclusion of a lost Preface, at the end of which was a flowered design similar to those on fol. 167*a*, 539*a*.

Date and Scribe. — No name or date is given, and there is no colophon at the end of the work; but judging from the style of the writing and the old cover bindings, the manuscript probably belongs to the late sixteenth or early seventeenth century. In either case the date can hardly be far removed from 1600 A.D.

Memorandums. — There are no Persian seals or memorandums; their absence may possibly be accounted for in part by the loss of the Preface, as noted in the next paragraph. There is, however, a marginal jotting in Turkish on fol. 39*a* recording that the order in a couplet, which is wrongly repeated on the next page, would be better if reversed; there is also a variant reading inserted on the margin of fol. 56*b* and the restoration of a verse omitted at the top of fol. 57*a*. On the fly-leaves there are pencil-notes of no importance.

Subject and Arrangement. — The epic down to the death of Alexander the Great. The manuscript once had a Preface, the conclusion of which can still be seen on the back of the first folio, which has had a page pasted over it, as explained above under 'Writing and Paper,' but the preceding part of this introduction has been lost. There are four great divisions of the poem, marked by illuminated half title-pages, as follows: I (fol. 1*b*–167*a*). First part. — II (fol. 167*b*–452*a*). 'Book of Kai Khusrau.' — III (fol. 452*b*–539*a*). 'Book of Bahman.' — IV (fol. 539*b*–579*a*). 'Book of Alexander.'

Illuminations and Illustrations. — There are four heavily adorned 'unwāns, or title-pieces, to introduce the several divisions of the poem, the predominating decoration being in gold and blue. The numerous small caption-bands that head the different sections of the epic narrative and occupy the space of two couplets in the two middle columns, are left uncolored, but are inscribed in gold letters, with the exception of the introductory one (fol. 1*b*) which is gold and is inscribed in light blue characters. Particularly graceful are the flowered designs at the close of the first division (fol. 167*a*) and the third division (fol. 539*a*); another one of these (fol. 1*a*), at the end of the practically lost Preface, occupied the back of the opening page, but has been pasted over, as explained above under 'Writing and Paper.' Gold sprinkling has been applied as an added embellishment on the two opening pages of the first two divisions of the poem (fol. 1*b*–2*a*; 167*b*–168*a*), as made in this manuscript.

There are twenty-eight large miniatures, each occupying most of the page. Their general style resembles that of the period to which the manuscript has been assigned above, and the Mongolian touch is still easily recognizable. No artist's name is found on any one, but a large number of them are plainly by the same painter, who in eight cases has added two banneret flags in the margin above the picture; a possible exception to such identity in manner of workmanship in the paintings so marked is found in the miniature on fol. 306*a*, which, although it has two banners, differs somewhat in style. In the case of the only two paintings which run over the side margins, namely fol. 220*a*, 375*a*, the work appears to be the execution of a single brush, though of still another artist; further proof of this is given by the beardless portrait of Rustam, as contrasted with all other representations of that hero in the book.

I (*a*) fol. 1*b*. Illuminated title-piece.

1 fol. 4*b*. Kaiūmarṣ, the first ruler of Īrān.

2 fol. 15*b*. Farīdūn overcomes Ḍaḥḥāk, the fiendish ruler of Babylon and Arabia, and imprisons him in chains on Mount Albūrz.

3 fol. 22*b*. Īraj slain by his brothers Tūr and Salm.

4 fol. 32*b*. The fabulous bird Sīmurgh brings back the youthful hero Zāl to his father Sām.

5 fol. 52*a*. The identification of this miniature is not quite certain. Apparently it represents a scene of anger between Mihrāb and his wife Sindukht, when he learned of their daughter's love for Zāl (Vullers, I. 180–184; tr. Warner, I. 284–287); but if so, the miniature is somewhat misplaced, as it is located in a passage describing a later incident, namely the birth of their daughter's child, the hero Rustam (Vullers, I. 223–224; tr. Warner, I. 320–321). If the subject be Rustam's birth, the representation seems inadequate in certain details.

6 fol. 69*a*. Rustam, though still a youth, attacks Afrāsiāb and lifts him from his saddle after Shamāsās had been slain by Qāran.

7 fol. 80*a*. Rustam kills the Dīv-i Safīd, or White Demon, in his cavern.

8 fol. 106*a*. Rustam lamenting over Suhrāb, whom he had slain, not knowing that the youth was his son.

9 fol. 116*a*. Siāwush passing through the fire-ordeal to prove his innocence of the calumnious charge of being in love with Sūdābah, his stepmother.

10 fol. 145*a*. Siāwush slain by Gurwī, the son of Zirah.

II (*b*) fol. 167*b*. Title-piece of the 'Book of Khusrau,' or second division of the poem made in this manuscript.

11 fol. 168*a*. Rustam and his father Zāl come to congratulate Kai Khusrau on becoming king.

12 fol. 208*a*. Rustam kills Ashkābūs with an arrow.

13 fol. 220*a*. Rustam captures the Khāqān of China.

14 fol. 250*b*. Rustam draws Bīzhan out of the pit into which the Dīvs had thrown him; the demons in rage watch from a distance.

15 fol. 283*a*. Rustam is about to kill Barzū, but learns from the latter's mother that Barzū is his grandson.

16 fol. 306*a*. Barzū lassoing Afrāsiāb.

17 fol. 320*a*. Hūmān slain by the hand of Bīzhan.

18 fol. 351*a*. Shīdah slain by Kai Khusrau.

19 fol. 375*a*. Kai Khusrau killing Afrāsiāb and his brother Garsīwaz.

20 fol. 419*b*. Asfandiār, with his lasso, pulls Gurgsār from his horse and takes him captive.

21 fol. 449*a*. Rustam shooting Asfandiār in the eyes with a two-pronged arrow.

III (*c*) fol. 452*b*. Title-piece of the 'Book of Bahman,' or third division in the manuscript.

22 fol. 486*a*. Rustam transfixes Shaghād with an arrow through the plane-tree just before he himself dies.

23 fol. 502*b*. Bahman, the son of Asfandiār, captures Farāmarz and puts him to death.

24 fol. 512*a*. An illustration of the story of how the poor man's cow frightened away the king's cow.

	25 fol. 538*a*.	Bahman killing a dragon.
IV	(*d*) fol. 539*b*.	Title-piece of the 'Book of Alexander,' or fourth division in the manuscript.
	26 fol. 550*a*.	Alexander at the death of Darius III, who was treacherously slain by two of his own officers.
	27 fol. 571*a*.	Alexander breaking bread with the Sage Khiḍr, at the Fountain of Life.
	28 fol. 578*a*.	Death of Alexander.

II

NIẒĀMĪ

NIẒĀMĪ

(1140–1203 A.D.)

Niẓāmī, the famous romantic poet of Persia, was born at the city of Ganjah, which corresponds to the modern Elizabetpol in Transcaucasia, and was the author of five long poetic works, each a masterpiece in the domain of the romantic epopee. The composition of these poems covered a period of more than thirty years, or approximately 1165–1198 A.D., and the collection is commonly grouped under the designation of *Khamsah*, 'Quintet,' or *Panj Ganj*, 'Five Treasures.' Some idea of the nature of these poems may be gleaned from their titles and the subjects treated.

(1) *Makhzan al-Asrār*, 'Treasure of Mysteries' (about 2300 couplets), a mystical poem rather than a romance, but brightened by numerous anecdotes poetically told.

(2) *Khusrau and Shīrīn* (about 7000 couplets), one of the best-known romantic Persian poems, telling the story of the Sāsānian King Khusrau Parwīz II (ruled 590–628 A.D.) and his love for the fair Shīrīn, together with the tragic fate of Shīrīn's devoted admirer, Farhād, the heroic artist-sculptor.

(3) *Lailā and Majnūn*, sometimes called the Persian Romeo and Juliet, a pathetic and romantic story (in some 4500 couplets) of the ideal love existing between the distraught Majnūn and the beauteous Beduin maid, Lailā, their union being finally brought about in Paradise.

(4) *Haft Paikar*, or *Bahrām-nāmah*, 'The Seven Effigies,' or 'The Story of Bahrām and the Seven Princesses,' a poetic composition (in some 5000 couplets), describing the adventures of the Sāsānian King Bahrām Gūr (ruled 420–438 A.D.), who discovered by chance on the walls of his palace the portraits of seven princesses, each the most beautiful daughter of a different ruler of the world. These he subsequently marries, and he visits them on seven successive days, from Saturday till Friday, in their seven different palaces, which are respectively decorated in a predominating color characteristic of the

nationality to which the princess belonged. Each princess in turn, during his visit, entertains him with some romantic tale.

(5) *Iskandar-nāmah*, 'Book of Alexander' (about 10,000 couplets) a legendary account of the exploits of Alexander the Great in Asia. Regarding this poem it may be noted that the manuscripts of Niẓāmī which preserve the work entire divide it into two separate parts, generally entitled: —

(*a*) *Sharaf-nāmah*, a long section narrating in romantic fashion the main events of Alexander's history.

(*b*) *Iqbāl-nāmah*, a somewhat fanciful presentation of notions (current in the Orient) regarding Alexander's views on wisdom and concerning his later exploits.

Sometimes, however, the first division is simply styled *Iskandar-nāmah*, and the second called *Khirad-nāmah-i Iskandarī*.

For details regarding Niẓāmī's life and works see E. G. Browne, *Literary History of Persia*, 2. 399–411, London and New York, 1906; I. Pizzi, *Storia della poesia persiana*, 2. 252-273, Turin, 1894; P. Horn, *Geschichte der persischen Litteratur*, p. 181–189, Leipzig, 1901; H. Ethé, *Neupersische Litteratur*, in Geiger and Kuhn's *Grundriss*, 2. 241–244. Partial translations of Niẓāmī's works are accessible in English and in other languages, *e.g.* by Atkinson, London, 1836 (reprinted several times); by F. v. Erdmann (Kazan, 1844); F. Rückert (Nuremberg, 1824); Wilberforce Clarke (London, 1885). Compare likewise W. Bacher, *Niẓāmī's Leben und Werke*, Leipzig, 1872; and Jackson, article 'Niẓāmī,' in Warner, *World's Best Literature*, New York, 1897.

6

Niẓāmī: Khamsah, 'Quintet,' or works complete. A richly illuminated manuscript of the middle of the fifteenth century (being dated 1449–1450 A.D.), remarkably well preserved, and containing thirty-one miniatures.

Size. — 10 × 6¼ in. (25.5 × 16.0 cm.); written surface, 7¼ × 4¼ in. (18.5 × 10.8 cm.). Folios 394, the last folio, also outlined with gold, being left blank to serve as a fly-leaf.

Binding. — Handsomely bound in heavy lacquer Persian binding, of a dark green color with borders of bronze gold and shaded lines. The outside covers are due apparently to a rebinding. The brown leather of the inside covers is older and may be contemporaneous with the age of the manuscript itself. The field of these in each case is of pressed leather with corner-angle designs and two small vignettes above and below an oblong medallion. This rich medallion is delicately cut to represent twice, upon a deep blue ground, a graceful Sīmurgh, a fabulous bird somewhat resembling the phoenix or bird of paradise.

Writing and Paper. — Written in a medium-sized Nasta'līq, of a handsome style, 19 lines to a page in four columns, ruled in gold with blue outline and an extra marginal ruling. The vellum paper is of fine quality, though of light weight, and has but slight sheen.

Date and Scribe. — The colophon gives the date as 853 A.H. = 1449–1450 A.D., but does not name the copyist.

Memorandums. — On the first and second fly-leaf and on folios 280*a*, 391*a*, 399*b* is stamped the seal of a former owner, Muḥammad Ḥusain, son of Muḥammad Ibrāhīm. On fol. 6*a* there are several impressions of this seal over each other. On the second fly-leaf is a didactic couplet in Turkish, and near it is a memorandum, also in Turkish, to the effect that the book is a Persian work. Adjoining this there is a brief note in Persian, but it has been so obliterated that a connected sense can not be made out of it. On the first fly-leaf there is an English signature 'Sidney I. A. Churchill.' On the last fly-leaf, beside some pencil memorandums in English, there is a printed plate, with the words: 'From the Library of Laurence W. Hodson, Compton Hall, near Wolverhampton.'

Subject and Arrangement. — The five poetical works of Niẓāmī complete and grouped as a Khamsah, or 'Quintet,' arranged as follows: — I. *Makhzan al-Asrār*, fol. 1*b*–32*b*. — II. *Khusrau u Shīrīn*, fol. 33*b*–117*b*. — III. *Lailā u Majnūn*, fol. 118*b*–183*a*. — IV. *Ḥaft Paikar*, fol. 183*b*–253*b*. — V. (*a*) First part of the *Book of Alexander*, here entitled *Sharaf-nāmah*, fol. 254*b*–346*a*. — (*b*) Second part of the *Book of Alexander*, here entitled *Iqbāl-nāmah*, fol. 346*b*–393*b*.

Illuminations and Illustrations. — The two illuminated introductory pages are highly ornate, as are the title-pieces to each of the five books; so also are the flowered and geometrical designs and gilded lettering at the close of each of the poems. In addition to the decorative bands as captions for the sections, there are frequent ornamental arrangements of verses written at an angle and embellished by tiny flowers. There are thirty-one miniatures, each occupying two-thirds of a page, though some are larger, and showing the style of the period of the Tīmūrids. They are apparently the work of two artists. <But Dr. Valentiner, *Bull. Met. Mus. of Art*, 8. 80, prefers to regard these miniatures as the work of a single brush — 'by an artist not of great refinement, but of vigor and entertaining variety. The design shows Chinese influence, still much in the style of the earlier Mongolian miniatures of the fourteenth century. The colors appear at first profuse

and almost offensive in their vividness, but a closer study shows them to be a nice expression of the artist's temperament, and not without brilliant ideas and imagination.'> [1] The chief details as to the subjects are as follows:—

I (*a*) fol. 1*a*. Ornate title-page with a medallion in the center, containing the names of Niẓāmī's five works; there are four angels at the corners of the page, as if making offerings.

(*b*) fol. 1*b*–2*a*. Two illuminated title-pages in blue and gold, the first giving the name of Niẓāmī's earliest work, *Makhzan al-Asrār*, and the second containing an invocation of blessing upon the author.

1 fol. 4*a*. Miniature illustrating Muḥammad's ascent to heaven in a vision.

2 fol. 15*a*. Anūshīrwān the Just (King Chosroes I, 531–579 A.D.) and his Vizir, who teaches the King a lesson from the talk he overheard between two owls.

II (*c*) fol. 33*b*. Illuminated 'unwān, or title-piece to Niẓāmī's second work, *Khusrau and Shīrīn.*

3 fol. 56*a*. Khusrau II (590–628 A.D.) kills a lion in Shīrīn's presence.

4 fol. 61*b*. Khusrau victorious over Bahrām Chūbīn.

5 fol. 76*b*. Shīrīn and her horse carried on the shoulders of her sculptor lover, Farhād.

6 fol. 87*a*. Khusrau arrives at Shīrīn's palace as she stands in the balcony. (The Arabic inscription under the balcony refers to the King.)

7 fol. 104*a*. Khusrau and Shīrīn united in wedlock.

III (*d*) fol. 118*b*. Decorative title-piece to *Lailā and Majnūn.*

8 fol. 130*b*. Lailā and Majnūn as children neglected their lessons to indulge in love-making.

9 fol. 135*a*. Majnūn's father takes the lovelorn youth on a pilgrimage to Mecca in hopes to restore his reason.

[1] Angles < > are used to indicate that the matter so inclosed is based on published material by Martin or by Valentiner that became accessible after 'copy' was ready to go to press.

10 fol. 142*a*. Naufal, the Arab chieftain, champions Majnūn's cause in battle.

11 fol. 147*b*. Majnūn gives himself as a prisoner to an old woman in order to release a man who was her captive.

12 fol. 154*b*. Majnūn mourns his father's death.

13 fol. 163*a*. Majnūn's mother visits him in the wilderness shortly before she dies.

14 fol. 173*b*. Lailā and Majnūn, long separated, swoon when they meet.

15 fol. 178*a*. Majnūn mourning at Lailā's tomb.

16 fol. 181*b*. Lailā and Majnūn united in Paradise, as seen in a vision by Zaid.

IV (*e*) fol. 183*b*. Decorative head-piece to the *Haft Paikar*.

17 fol. 202*b*. Bahrām Gūr transfixes a deer's foot to its ear with an arrow in the presence of his sweetheart Fitnah, who plays the harp. (Reference has been made above to this story also in Firdausī.)

18 fol. 209*b*. Bahrām and the Indian Princess in the Black Palace on Saturday.

19 fol. 217*a*. Bahrām and the Chinese (?) Princess in the Yellow Palace on Sunday.

20 fol. 220*b*. Bahrām and the Khwārazmian (?) Princess in the Green Palace on Monday.

21 fol. 224*b*. Bahrām and the Russian Princess in the Red Palace on Tuesday.

22 fol. 228*a*. Bahrām and the Persian Princess in the Turquoise Palace on Wednesday.

23 fol. 234*b*. Bahrām and the Moorish (?) Princess in the Sandal Palace on Thursday.

24 fol. 240*a*. Bahrām and the Byzantine Princess in the White Palace on Friday.

V^A (*f*) fol. 254*b*. Decorative head-piece to the First Section of the *Book of Alexander* — the section being here entitled *Sharaf-nāmah*.

25 fol. 270*b*. Battle between Alexander and the Zangīs (Ethiopians or Egyptians).

26 fol. 294*b*. Alexander and the daughter of Darius III united in marriage.

27 fol. 322*a*. Discussion in Alexander's presence about the difference between Occidental and Oriental art. The Byzantine and Chinese painters vie in a trial of skill, and the former use mirrors (shown in the side panels of the picture) to reflect the art of the latter.

28 fol. 332*b*. Alexander's combat against the Russians.

29 fol. 342*b*. Alexander visits the Land of Darkness in search of the Fountain of Life.

VB (*g*) fol. 346*b*. Decorative title-piece to the Second Section of the *Book of Alexander*, here called *Iqbāl-nāmah*.

30 fol. 358*b*. Alexander and the Seventy Wise Men of Greece.

31 fol. 384*a*. Alexander's return from the East to the North and his shutting out Gog and Magog by a wall.

7

Niẓāmī: Khamsah, 'Quintet,' or works complete. A handsome manuscript of the beginning of the sixteenth century, being dated 1509–1510 A.D., with richly illuminated introductory pages and title-pieces and with nineteen miniatures.

Size. — $11\frac{1}{2} \times 7$ in. (29.2×17.8 cm.); written space, $7\frac{7}{8} \times 4$ in. (19.6×10.4 cm.). Folios 357; one leaf is missing between folios 164 and 165, and one between folios 311 and 312.

Binding. — Original Persian flap-binding of dark maroon leather heavily embossed with gold. The ornamentation on both of the outer covers is alike and shows a field decorated with an elaborate tendril design impressed upon the leather and gilded. This is framed by a border of flowered panels and is inclosed by a narrow gold band in the style of a Grecian border. In two long gilded panels above and below the inner field there is beautifully stamped a quotation from Niẓāmī's dedication of his *Makhzan al-Asrār* to Fakhr ad-

Dīn Bahrām-Shāh (see fol. 8*a* of the manuscript). They relate to the mystic power of the Word, or Divine Revelation :—

'There is nothing superior to the Word (Revelation).
The fortune of this world depends only upon the Word;
As long as the sound of a word exists,
May Niẓāmī's name remain fresh through the word.'

The inner covers present a good example of the typical combination of cut-out leather work and blind pressing common in ornamental Persian bindings. The main design is given by a figure of dull red leather laid upon a blue ground, the central feature being a large medallion with a pendant above and below it, and outlined with an artistic and intricate pattern of gold and black tracery. The corner angles and side-pieces are similar, and the whole has a double gold cording as a border. The flap cover is identical with the other two in all details.

Writing and Paper. — Small Nasta'līq hand of fine quality, 21 lines to a page in four gold-ruled columns, with gold and blue outline. The paper is of medium weight, cream-colored, and has a slight sheen. The fly-leaves are of a different quality and are modern, being due to a repairing of the binding.

Date and Scribe. — The two dates given by the scribe show that the copying of the manuscript occupied more than four months. At the end of fol. 31*a*, when the transcribing of the *Makhzan al-Asrār* was completed, he noted the date as 'the twentieth of Jumāda II in the year nine hundred and fifteen [= Oct. 5, 1509 A.D.].' In the colophon on fol. 357*a* he gives the day of completing the work as 'Ṣalaṣa 24 Shawwāl in the year nine hundred and fifteen [= Tuesday, Feb. 4, 1510 A.D.].' He adds his name as Na'īm ad-Dīn, the Scribe. No place is mentioned, but undoubtedly this is the same person as Na'īm ad-Dīn, the Scribe, of Shīrāz,

NAUFAL, THE ARAB CHIEFTAIN, CHAMPIONING THE CAUSE OF MAJNŪN
Ms. No. 7, fol. 130*a* (see page 56)

who nine years earlier (August 7, 1501) finished copying another manuscript of Niẓāmī's *Khamsah*, cf. Sachau and Ethé, *Cat. Pers. Mss. Bodl. Lib.*, col. 490, no. 587.

Memorandums. — On the blank side of the first folio near the top there is a Persian memorandum taken from the illuminated head-line of the next page, 'the method of stringing of pearls,' and thus indicating that the work is a poetical one. Below is a memorandum in Arabic recording that the book was 'owned by Ismā'īl 'Āṣim, son of Chalabī Zādah, the Governor, who had a valiant, brilliant, pure, and victorious administration. May God Almighty maintain his rank, and respect his justice!' Some obliterated Persian words in another jotting indicate that the name of a former owner has been erased. On p. 8 is impressed a seal containing the imperial monogram and date of 'Sulṭān Aḥmad, 1115 A.H. [= 1703 A.D.],' showing that the book once belonged to that Turkish ruler. A small oval seal on the last page has been obliterated so that it cannot be read.

Subject and Arrangement. — The five poetic romances of Niẓāmī as described above: — I. *Makhzan al-Asrār*, fol. 1*b*–31*a*. — II. *Khusrau u Shīrīn*, fol. 31*b*–108*b*. — III. *Lailā u Majnūn*, fol. 109*b*–164*b*. — IV. *Haft Paikar*, fol. 165*a* (preceding fol. lost)–228*a*. — V. (*a*) *Book of Alexander*, first portion, here entitled *Sharaf-nāmah*, fol. 229*b*–311*b*. — (*b*) Second portion of same, or *Iqbāl-nāmah*, occupies fol. 311*b*–357*a*, but the decorative title-piece is missing, owing to the loss of the folio between 311 and 312.

Illuminations and Illustrations. — In addition to the richly illuminated title-pieces introducing the separate books, there are decorative bands as captions to the sections of each poem with numerous ornamental floweret designs and nineteen fine miniatures in the style of the Ṣafavid period to illustrate the work. They seem, as a whole, to be the work of a single artist, and in size they average about three-quarters of a page. <Miniature no. 7 has been selected for reproduction by Valentiner, *Bull. Metropol. Museum of Art*, 8. 83.> The subjects are as follows: —

I (a^1–a^2) fol. 1*b*–3*a*. Two exquisitely illuminated introductory pages to *Makhzan al-Asrār* with rich colors of blue and gold, and showing four ornate medallions that give the name of Niẓāmī as author and praise him in highest terms.

1 fol. 16*a*. An old widowed woman complains to Sulṭān Sanjar of ill-treatment by one of his officers.

II (*b*) fol. 31*b*. Illuminated title-piece to *Khusrau and Shīrīn.*

2 fol. 46*b*. King Khusrau catches sight of Shīrīn bathing in a pool.

3 fol. 72*b*. Shīrīn goes to see the wonderful rock-carvings (near Kirmānshāh) by the sculptor Farhād, her admirer. (In the tiny pictures on the rocks in the painting is the rimed couplet: 'If you had real love for Shīrīn, you would not see her picture in the eyes of men.')

4 fol. 81*b*. Khusrau comes to the Palace of Shīrīn as she stands in the balcony window. (The arabesque inscription over the doorway calls him 'the Just King.')

5 fol. 95*b*. Khusrau and Shīrīn united in wedlock. (The arabesque over the door is the same as the preceding.)

III (*c*) fol. 109*b*. Illuminated title-piece to *Lailā and Majnūn.*

6 fol. 120*a*. As children Lailā and Majnūn neglect their studies to devote their hearts to each other.

7 fol. 130*a*. Naufal, the Arab chieftain, champions in battle the cause of the love-distraught Majnūn. <Now reproduced in *Bull. Metropol. Museum of Art*, 8. 83.>

8 fol. 133*b*. An old woman leads in chains the lovelorn Majnūn, who has sacrificed himself to free a man whom she had taken prisoner.

King Khusrau seated on his Throne

Painting by Mīrak, Ms. No. 8, fol. 64*a* (see page 65)

9 fol. 156*b*. The chaste meeting of Lailā and Majnūn. Both swoon at seeing each other after their long separation.

IV [(*d*) fol. between 164 and 165 missing. Decorative title-page to *Haft Paikar* is thereby lost.]

10 fol. 180*b*. Bahrām Gūr saves his crown by killing two lions.

11 fol. 184*b*. Bahrām Gūr's sweetheart, Fitnah ('Mischief'), performs the feat of climbing a ladder with a cow on her shoulder. (This incident is a familiar story in the Persian accounts of Bahrām.) The inscription on the door calls him 'the Just King.'

12 fol. 196*a*. Bahrām visits the Princess of the Yellow Palace on Sunday.

13 fol. 202*a*. Bahrām visits the Russian Princess in the Red Palace on Tuesday. (The title 'the Just King' is seen in the inscription over the doors.)

14 fol. 221*b*. Bahrām learns a lesson about his unfaithful vizir from the action of an old shepherd who punished his sheep-dog that was unfaithful to the charge of the flocks.

V^A (*e*) fol. 228*b*. Decorative head-piece to the First Section of the *Book of Alexander*, here called *Sharaf-nāmah-i Iskandarī*. There is no title-piece to the Second Section (or *Iqbāl*), as the folio that contained it is missing between folios 311 and 312.

15 fol. 258*b*. Death of Darius III (Dārā) in the presence of Alexander, who then leads to execution the two treacherous assassins of the monarch.

16 fol. 271*b*. Alexander, disguised as a legate, visits Queen Nūshābah, who recognizes him and proves the fact by his portrait, which she had.

17 fol. 291*b*. Alexander's visit to the Khāqān of China.

V^B [(*f*) The decorative title-piece to the Second Section of the *Book of Alexander* is missing through the loss, already noted, of a folio between 311–312.]

18 fol. 318*a*. Alexander learns from a shepherd the gate by which to enter the city. ('The Just King' is inscribed over the door.)

19 fol. 330*a*. Alexander consulting the Seven Wise Men.

8

Niẓāmī : Khamsah, or works complete. A magnificent manuscript of the early sixteenth century, being dated as completed in 1525 A.D., and copied by the famous calligraphist Sulṭān Muḥammad Nūr; it is adorned with fifteen exquisite miniatures, specimens of the finest workmanship of the contemporary Bahzād school. <These masterpieces are now assigned by Martin, *Miniature Painting*, vol. 1, p. 52, to the renowned Mīrak, 'the Carpaccio of the East,' who ranks highest among all Persian painters except Bahzād, and appears to have been a pupil of that teacher. Regarding this superb codex, which came from the library of the Ṣafavid kings of Persia and was among the treasures of the later Shāhs, Dr. Martin writes that it 'is second to none of the same period; there are certainly larger ones in existence, but none of finer quality, with such a profusion of architecture and such charming colouring; furthermore, it is in perfect condition, and in a splendid contemporary binding.' Cf. also Martin, *op. cit.*, 1. 116.> Particularly noticeable also is the gold-frosted paper with a different marginal color for each of the five romantic poems. The original flap-cover binding furnishes a fine example of Persian art in that line of production.

Size. — $12\frac{3}{4} \times 8\frac{3}{4}$ in. (32.6×22.4 cm.); written space, $7 \times 4\frac{3}{4}$ in. (17.8×12.0 cm.). Folios 368. There are missing one folio between 89 and 90 and two folios between 176 and 177.

Binding. — Original Persian flap-binding of brown leather highly decorated. The outside covers, and the flap to match, are gilded and elegantly embossed with scenes comprising trees, deer, hares, monkeys, storks, wild ducks, a dragon, and the fabulous Sīmurgh bird. The inside covers, including the interior of the flap, are equally beautiful, and furnish, for the period to which the manuscript belongs, a fine example of the Oriental bookbinder's art in applying exquisitely cut-out leather designs upon a background of color. In each case the inner field presents a rich blue basis embellished by a delicately perforated central medallion of gilded and bronzed leather, with smaller vignettes of similar traceries above and below it; and surrounding this is a pressed leather design of a deep red color, set off by corner angles filled with a network of kindred gold and brown traceries cut out of the leather. The whole inner field in these is framed by a narrow gold border with a running tendril design. The outer margin of the field is peculiarly ornate, as it consists of a series of light blue panels interrupted by olive green vignettes, and each of these panels contains a Persian verse most delicately tooled in the leather and gilded.

The contents of these verses in the panels beginning at the upper right-hand corner of the front cover and reading to the left and then down is as follows: —

Front cover (beginning in the upper right corner).

Panel 1. 'This book is an ornament of the page of time.

Panel 2. The merit of the book is suited to the quality of the reader.

Panel 3. For each small detail of it the artist has procured limpid gold.

Panel 4. The sky became mother of pearl, the sun was made Saturn,

Panel 5. By the cover bound upon its soft face.

Panel 6. For lovers each leaf (of the book) is a new chapter.

Panel 7. Its composition is a Treasury of the Secrets of Wisdom — (*Makhzan al-Asrār*).

Panel 8. In wisdom the book is deeper than the pearl of pure water.

Panel 9. It is the perfect verse of an intimate friend.

Panel 10. It brings a hundred ideas, but speaks only that which is true.

Back cover (beginning at the top).

Panel 11. Sometimes the tongue of the lovelorn lover (*i.e.* Khusrau) speaks;

Panel 12. At other times a charming word from the lips of the beloved (*i.e.* Shīrīn) is unveiled;

Panel 13. It scatters sweetness over the memory of *Khusrau and Shīrīn.*

Panel 14. It describes the story of *Lailā and Majnūn* as a pearl of pure water.

Panel 15. It gives a description of *Iskandar* (Alexander the Great),

Panel 16. And of how he ultimately left this ruined world;

Panel 17. Finally it explains his kindness and virtues.

Panel 18. Beyond measure and great is the amount

Panel 19. Of the beautiful writing on its rose leaves;

Panel 20. It is a rare picture delineated, as it were, by the pen of Providence upon the water.

Flap cover—side (beginning in the lower right corner).

Panel 21. May these beautiful pages and their unparalleled script

Panel 22. Grant light to the pupil of the eye of the Writer;

Panel 23. And with it sweet virtues and comfort.

Panel 24. The veil is raised from his face, in hope

Panel 25. That from the Asaf of the time he may obtain a glance and may gain

Flap cover—back.

Panel 26. From that glance everlasting joy.

Panel 27. By the gift of God may the prosperity of his fortune be everlasting;

Panel 28. And may the prayers from the lips of the people be accepted.'

Writing and Paper.—The writing is a beautiful Nasta'līq of a medium size and is worthy of the renown of the eminent calligraphist Sulṭān Muḥammad Nūr, who executed it, as stated below. It may be worth noting that the letter *jīm* is written throughout instead of *chīm*. The paper is of a remarkable quality, heavy in weight, and the portions of

King Khusrau and his Bride Shīrīn
Painting by Mirak, Ms. No. 8, fol. 104*b* (see page 65)

the pages containing the writing are so skilfully inset into the borders as almost to defy detection, yet the fact that they are inset is proved by such a folio as 143. At basis both insets and borders are a laid paper, pressure having probably been applied to give the smooth finish; the borders are slightly heavier and more opaque than the inset page. For each poem a different colored paper, always in perfect harmony with the miniatures, has been employed: (1) rich cream, (2) salmon pink, (3) saffron yellow, (4) delicate blue, (5) light cream. The whole is richly sprinkled with flakes of gold, the written portion of the page being sprinkled more delicately, so as not to interfere with the writing.

Date and Scribe. — The date of completion of the copying is given in the colophon as 931 A.H. = 1524–1525 A.D. The same year, Rajab 931 A.H. = April–May, 1525, is found also inserted in the inscription across the miniature on fol. 104*b*, as noted below. The name of the scribe is given in the colophon, where the copyist speaks of the work as being 'finished with God's help by the hand of the poor and obscure Sulṭān Muḥammad Nūr.' This well-known calligraphist was the son of the famous penman Mashhadī, and was a pupil of his father, who lived at the court of Tamerlane's great-grandson, the Sulṭān Ḥusain Bāiqarā (who ruled at Herāt, 1469–1506). Muḥammad Nūr was a contemporary of the celebrated miniaturist Bahzād and is known to have copied a poem by Jāmī in 900 A.H. = 1494 A.D., and was himself something of a poet. Furthermore, it is important to add that the name of still another famous penman, Maḥmūd, is inserted in an inscription in a miniature, on fol. 213*a*, referring to the gilding and the handwriting in the miniature on that particular page as being 'entirely the work of Maḥmūd.' This Maḥmūd was likewise one of the pupils of Mashhadī and was an eminent master of calligraphy and gilding, in the time of the Ṣafavid monarch Shāh Isma'īl (d. 1524). Shāh Isma'īl, on going to war with the Turkish sultan Salīm I, is stated to have left Maḥmūd and Bahzād at home, saying, 'If I am conquered I do not wish Shāh Maḥmūd of Nīshāpūr (his court calligraphist) and Master Bahzād (the miniaturist) to fall into the hands of the enemy.' Maḥmūd's death occurred about the year 1545 A.D. For some account of the persons mentioned see Huart, *Les Calligraphes et les miniaturistes de l'Orient musulman*, p. 221–226, Paris, 1908; cf. also Sachau and Ethé, *Cat. Pers. Mss. Bodl. Lib.*, col. 623, no. 918; <compare now likewise Martin, *Miniature Painting*, 1. 41; the reference, moreover, which Martin (*op. cit.*, 1. 117, ll. 3–6) makes to a manuscript written in 1502 by Shāh Maḥmūd may well be connected with the Maḥmūd who has been mentioned already as signing his name in the arabesque inscription on fol. 213*a*.>

Memorandums. — On the back of the first folio is a memorandum in Persian stating: 'This book, the Khamsah of Niẓāmī, is the gift of his Majesty, my father; it came into the library of his Highness, the noble Shāhzādah Sulṭān Ḥusain Mīrzā, in the month of Zīḥajjah 1260 A.H. [= Dec., 1844 A.D.].' Below this, twice repeated, and also on the last folio is stamped the oval seal of Sulṭān Ḥusain. This governor-prince, Shāhzādah Sulṭān Ḥusain Mīrzā, must have been (judging from the date) Prince Ḥusain 'Alī Mīrzā, a son of the Persian monarch Fatḥ 'Alī Shāh, and Governor of the Province of Shīrāz (consult Ker Porter, *Travels in Persia*, 1. 692; 2. 508, London, 1821–1822). <So also Martin, *Miniature Painting*, 1. 116, ll. 9–11.> The seals of other owners are obliterated, as is also the stamp of a round seal (probably of the first owner) which had been impressed at the top of every folio throughout the book.

On fol. 178*a* is a small square seal, the signet of Hidāyat, who combines in his seal the Arabic phrase *min hudā*, 'from [God's] guidance,' choosing the latter word as akin to his name Hidāyat. It may be noted that there was a Persian literary historian named Hidāyat Riḍā Qulī Khān who died in 1871 A.D., according to Ethé, *Neupersische Litteratur*, in Geiger and Kuhn's *Grundriss der iranischen Philologie*, 2. 314. Furthermore, on the margin of fol. 114*a* are two brief phrases of benediction where the name of Muḥammad occurs in the text. There are also marginal corrections or additions of omissions in the text on fol. 162*a*, 197*a*, 221*b*, 222*a*.

Subject and Arrangement. — The complete works of Niẓāmī, arranged as follows: — I. *Makhzan al-Asrār*, fol. 1*b*–32*b*. — II. *Khusrau u Shīrīn*, fol. 33*b*–116*a*. — III. *Lailā u Majnūn*, fol. 117*b*–178*a*. — IV. *Haft Paikar*, fol. 179*b*–246*b*. — V. *Book of Alexander*, the sections being entitled (*a*) *Kitāb-i Iskandar-nāmah*, fol. 247*b*–328*b*, and (*b*) *Khirad-nāmah-i Iskandarī*, fol. 329*b*–368*a*.

Illuminations and Illustrations. — The two elegantly illuminated first pages, or 'unwāns, with headlines and footlines in Kufic style of script, are particularly fine, as are also the ornate smaller headings of the separate books with titles in Persian script. To lend a decorative effect, as in other Persian manuscripts, the writing is often done at an angle and inclosed in parallelograms. Throughout the work there are likewise chapter captions in gold.

The fifteen exquisite miniatures in the codex are in the finest style of the contemporary school of Bahzād, of the early sixteenth century. <They are now decisively assigned by Martin, 1. 52 (see above), to Mīrak, the greatest pupil of Bahzād, it is believed. Mīrak came from Isfahān and began his work at Herāt, in Bahzād's later years; and as

a painter, peerless in his way, he is considered to be the founder or reformer of the school of art that is now called after the city of Bukhārā. His miniatures, though few exist, are recognized to be supreme of their kind. His wonderful skill of execution, his balance in grouping, his sense of color, and his specially refined touch in all that relates to architecture, entitle his delicate paintings to praise of the highest kind. The date when this master lived was approximately 1475–1545. Five plates from the manuscript here described are to be found in Martin, 2. pl. 96–99.>[1]

Originally our present codex had sixteen miniatures, as shown by the Persian number given to each, but one of them (No. 5) is missing. The two illuminated introductory title-pages, or ʻunwāns, with headlines and footlines in Kufic style of script, are particularly fine, as are also the superb smaller headings of the separate books with titles in Persian script. Throughout the work there are chapter captions in gold. Details are as follows: —

I	(*a–b*)	fol. 1*a*–2*b*.	Two ornate title-pages to the work and forming the introduction to the *Makhzan al-Asrār*.
	1	fol. 17*a*.	An old woman complains to Sulṭān Sanjar about an injustice committed by one of his officers.
II	(*c*)	fol. 33*b*.	Illuminated title-piece to *Khusrau and Shīrīn*.
	2	fol. 50*a*.	Khusrau catches sight of the fair Shīrīn as she is bathing in a pool.

[1] <Martin (*op. cit.*, 2. pl. 99*a*, left) reproduces another of Mīrak's paintings, taken from a manuscript of the Eastern Turkish poet Nawā'ī, which was completed two years later than the present manuscript, as it was dated in 1527 A.D.; that miniature (Bahrām in the Dark Palace) closely resembles the one painted by Mīrak on the same subject in this copy, fol. 213*a*, see below.>

BAHRAM GŪR IN THE SANDAL PALACE

Painting by Mirak, Ms. No. 8, fol. 230*b* (see page 66)

3 fol. 64*a*. Khusrau seated upon his throne. <Now reproduced in Martin, 2. pl. 97*a*, left.>

4 fol. 74*a*. Shīrīn goes to see the wonderful mountain sculpture of her artist admirer Farhād, who has turned the course of a stream from out of the rocks.

[5 fol., with miniature, missing, between fol. 89–90. Judging from the context this picture must have related to the coming of Khusrau to the castle of Shīrīn.]

6 fol. 104*b*. Marriage of Khusrau and Shīrīn. (The Persian inscription beautifully written in white letters across the upper part of the miniature reads as follows: — 'This inscription was written in Rajab 931 A.H. [=April–May, 1525 A.D.]. This soul-refreshing, delightsome, and most perfect vaulted recess is neither small nor large, but it is a lofty chamber of nuptial bliss, a soul-inspiring recess, a heart-entrancing mansion, a place of delightsome air, a most perfect abode; the roses in this palace have blossomed out as Shīrīn; the mole on her cheek is like rosewater and sugar.' Below this, in the center, above the window, is an invocation to God, 'O thou Opener of Doors!') <Now reproduced in Martin, 2. pl. 98*b*, right.>

III (*d*) fol. 117*b*. Illuminated title-piece to *Lailā and Majnūn.*

7 fol. 129*a*. Lailā and Majnūn in love with each other at school. (Note the two boys playing ball in the court outside the school in the lower left-hand panel.) In an arabesque verse written in white letters over the portal are the lines: —

'O teacher, give no instruction of an unjust kind
to that fairy-faced girl (*i.e.* Lailā),
Nor anything but good; for nothing else is
worthy of that beauteous face.'

IV (*e*) fol. 179*b*. Illuminated title-piece to *Haft Paikar.*

8 fol. 207*a*. Bahrām Gūr in the Dark Palace on Saturday. The white arabesque inscription reads: — 'Happy is that assembly where the royal seat is

placed. And bright is that mansion over which the moon is passing.' (The reference is respectively to Bahrām and the Princess.) <Now reproduced in Martin, 2. pl. 99*b*, right.>

9 fol. 213*a*. Bahrām Gūr in the Yellow Palace on Sunday. The arabesque inscription is interesting as containing an allusion to the delineator Maḥmūd, as mentioned above in connection with the scribe. It reads in substance as follows: 'The command regarding this gold-encrusted dome has been obeyed, and the inscription, which is added, is altogether the work of Maḥmūd.' (The lower left-hand figure in the picture is probably a dancing-boy with curls).

10 fol. 216*b*. Bahrām Gūr in the Green Palace on Monday. The inscription over the doorway reads: 'Over the emerald portico is inscribed in gold: "Nothing but the goodness of the generous remains."' <Now reproduced in Martin, 2. pl. 97*b*, right.>

11 fol. 220*a*. Bahrām Gūr in the Red Palace on Tuesday. Over the left-hand doorway is an invocation to God, 'O thou Opener of Doors!'

12 fol. 224*b*. Bahrām Gūr in the Turquoise Palace on Wednesday. Over the pavilion is written: 'The foundation of this turquoise dome they have laid and have made a place to entertain the lovers together.'

13 fol. 230*b*. Bahrām Gūr in the Sandal Palace on Thursday. <Now reproduced in Martin, 2. pl. 98*a*, left, and in *Bulletin Metropol. Mus. of Art*, 8. 81.>

14 fol. 235*b*. Bahrām Gūr in the White Palace on Friday. The inscription reads: 'My eye had slight ambition and that even has been washed away by tears. I have therefore made this house for thee plain white throughout.'

V^A (*f*) fol. 247*b*. Illuminated title-piece to the First Section of the *Book of Alexander*, here entitled *Kitāb-i Iskandar-nāmah*.

15 fol. 279*a*. Battle between Iskandar and Dārā, or Alexander the Great and Darius III.

16 fol. 321*b*. Alexander receives the booty on the day of battle. <Now reproduced in *Bulletin Metropol. Mus. of Art*, 8. 85.>

V[B] (*g*) fol. 329*b*. Illuminated title-piece to the Second Section of the *Book of Alexander*, here entitled *Khirad-nāmah-i Iskandarī*, or 'Alexander-Book of Wisdom.'

9

Niẓāmī: **Khamsah**, or works complete as a 'Quintet.' A manuscript of about the middle of the sixteenth century, illuminated by five finely executed double title-pages to the separate poems, including the two subdivisions of the last romance, all of them being of full size; there is likewise a single introductory title-page of half size, belonging to a later date. The manuscript is illustrated by miniatures, mostly three-quarter-page in size.

Size. — $11\frac{1}{2} \times 8$ in. (29.2×21.3 cm.); written space, $8\frac{7}{8} \times 5\frac{3}{4}$ in. (22.5×14.5 cm.). Folios 279; the last page, fol. 279*b*, is left blank. There are six folios missing at the beginning, the *Makhzan al-Asrār* here opening with the praise of the Word, or Divine Revelation (cf. ed. Bland, p. 21); the upper half of this first page has been re-pasted and a new 'unwān, or title-piece, prepared for it.

Binding. — Red Persian morocco covers of a later date, pressed and with decorative gilt stamping. In rebinding the pages have been trimmed so that many of the catchwords at the bottom of the folios have been cut off.

Writing and Paper. — Medium-sized Naskhī style of writing, 25 lines to a page in four gold-ruled columns, with gold and blue outlinings. A peculiarity of the scribe is occasionally to extend the tail of the Persian letter for *t* to a distance considerably beyond the marginal ruling of the left side of the page. Worthy of mention is the elegant use of the Kufic script in all the title-pages except the first, which is of a later date, as already explained. The paper is of a rather heavy quality, creamish in color, and has considerable sheen.

Date and Scribe. — Neither is given, but the date of the manuscript is approximately the middle of the sixteenth century.

Memorandums. — On the back of the last fly-leaf is a Persian jotting which states that the copy was 'bought on the fourth day of the week (*i.e.* Wednesday), the second of the month of Sha'bān, year 9 [*erasure*]'; and adds: 'Ours till it passes (?) to you (?).' On folio 115*a* there is the seal of an owner 'Ṣāliḥ . . . 1177 A.H. [= 1763–1764 A.D.].'

Subject and Arrangement. — The five romantic poems of Niẓāmī, previously described, arranged as follows: — I. *Makhzan al-Asrār*, fol. 1*b*–20*a*. (Owing to the loss of six folios at the beginning, this portion opens with the praise of the Word, cf. ed. Bland, p. 21.) — II. *Khusrau u Shīrīn*, fol. 20*b*–84*a*. — III. *Lailā u Majnūn*, fol. 84*b*–127*a*. — IV. *Haft Paikar*, fol. 127*b*–179*a*. — V. (*a*) First portion of the *Book of Alexander*, here entitled *Kitāb-i Sharaf-nāmah*, fol. 179*b*–244*a*. — (*b*) Second portion of the *Book of Alexander*, here entitled *Kitāb-i Iqbāl-nāmah*, fol. 244*b*–279*a*.

Illuminations and Illustrations. — The 'unwāns (except the first, which is of later date, as already noted) are double pages throughout, and are particularly fine in design and execution. Note has already been made of the Kufic style of writing in which the title or subject of the special poem is recorded on these pages. There are also frequent illuminated cap-

ALEXANDER THE GREAT RECEIVING BOOTY ON THE DAY OF BATTLE
Painting by Mīrak, Ms. No. 8, fol. 321*b* (see page 67)

tions, with gold lettering, as headings to different sections. The miniatures, eighteen in number, generally occupy three-quarters of a page, though some are smaller, and show strong evidence of the Mongol influence. In style they resemble those in the manuscript of Niẓāmī's Haft Paikar (No. 5), but belong to an earlier period. They appear to be the work of a single artist, or possibly two, though no name is mentioned. Details as to the subjects are as follows:

I (*a*) fol. 1*b*. Half-page illuminated title to *Makhzan al-Asrār*, with a foliated design. As previously observed, this half-page introductory decoration differs in size and style from the double title-pages of the other four books and is inferior to them, having been added when that upper half of the page was repaired, as is shown by the pasting.

1 fol. 8*a*. Sulṭān Sanjar is appealed to by an old woman to redress a flagrant injustice inflicted by one of his officers.

II (*b–c*) fol. 20*b*–21*a*. Two illuminated title-pages to *Khusrau and Shīrīn*.

2 fol. 30*b*. Khusrau's picture presented to Shīrīn. (The painter is peeping from the background above, as the maid presents the portrait.)

3 fol. 34*b*. Khuṣrau catches sight of Shīrīn bathing.

4 fol. 40*b*. Khusrau and Shīrīn playing polo — he on his famous steed 'Black as Night,' she on her palfrey 'Rose-roan.'

5 fol. 64*a*. Khusrau and Shīrīn meet in her bower.

6 fol. 75*b*. Khusrau and Shīrīn united in wedlock.

7 fol. 79*b*. Death of Khusrau by treachery.

III (*d–e*) fol. 84*b*–85*a*. Two illuminated title-pages to *Lailā and Majnūn*.

8 fol. 94*b*. Lailā and Majnūn, in love at school, devote themselves to each other. (In the picture is shown how Majnūn has left the boys and has come over to the girls' side of the school.)

9	fol. 104*b*.	Combat between Majnūn's friend Naufal, the Arab, and the tribe of Lailā.
10	fol. 111*b*.	Majnūn gives himself as a prisoner to an old woman in order to release a captive of hers.
IV (*f–g*)	fol. 127*b*–128*a*.	Two illuminated title-pages to *Haft Paikar*.
11	fol. 136*b*.	Bahrām Gūr hunting. (The lion's chap is pierced by the arrow.)
12	fol. 143*a*.	Bahrām Gūr exhibits his skill with the bow to his favorite, Fitnah ('Mischief'), by transfixing the deer's foot to its ear. (This familiar story has been referred to above.)
13	fol. 156*a*.	Bahrām Gūr and the Princess of the Green Palace.
V[A] (*h–i*)	fol. 179*b*–180*a*.	Two illuminated title-pages to the first section of the *Iskandar-nāmah*, or *Book of Alexander*, the title being here given as *Kitāb-i Sharaf-nāmah.*
14	fol. 192*b*.	Alexander in combat with the King of the Zangīs (Egyptians or Ethiopians).
15	fol. 209*b*.	Alexander weds the daughter of Darius III.
16	fol. 216*a*.	Alexander, disguised as an envoy, before Queen Nūshābah.
17	fol. 219*a*.	Alexander in search of the Fountain of Life in the Land of Darkness, meets Khiḍr, the Sage of Eternal Youth.
V[B] (*j–k*)	fol. 244*b*–245*a*.	Two illuminated title-pages of the second section of the *Iskandar-nāmah*, here called *Kitāb-i Iqbāl-nāmah*.
18	fol. 260*b*.	Alexander and the circle of the Seven Sages.

10

Niẓāmī: Haft Paikar, or 'Seven Portraits,' the fourth of Niẓāmī's five romantic poems, and comprised in a manuscript of great interest and value. This particular copy is a royal volume, as it was specially presented to the Mughal Emperor Akbar the Great and belonged later to his grandson Shāh Jahān. The colophon is dated 1580 A.D., <but the body of the manuscript must be years earlier, as explained below.> This book from the library of the Mughals is handsomely illuminated, and is adorned by five beautiful full-page miniatures <signed by Bahzād, the most famous Persian artist, who lived about 1460–1525.> From Akbar's chronicles it is known that the poetic romances of Niẓāmī, of which this volume forms a part, were among the favorite books of that great emperor.[1]

Size. — 11 × 7 in. (28.0 × 18.0 cm.); written space, $7\frac{3}{4} \times 4\frac{3}{4}$ in. (19.7 × 12.0 cm.). Folios 56, numbered in Persian figures at the top of the right-hand columns, and recorded also in a memorandum in Persian on the last page near Shāh Jahān's seal; but folios 29 and 35 are missing.

Binding. — Lacquer covers, adorned both inside and outside with scenes introducing wild animals, birds, flowers, and trees. There are evidences of rebinding and repair.

Writing and Paper. — Elegant Nasta'līq hand, 25 lines to a page, in four gold-ruled columns with outlinings in gold and blue. All the pages are inset, or rather have been re-inset, in a pink-hued paper, the insets being of a heavier and better quality than the borders, and having a *café au lait* tinge.

[1] See Abu'l Faḍl, *Ā'īn-i Akbarī, or Institutes of Akbar*, translated by F. Gladwin, I. 113, London, 1800.

is furnished by the seals on the last page, containing the name of Akbar and his grandson Shāh Jahān, and by the memorandums adjoining these signets. The chronological order of these appears to be as follows: —

The seal (1) of Akbar (combined with the name of Muḥib 'Alī) is stamped near the lower right-hand corner of the last page; it reads: 'Akbar Shāh — his servant Muḥib 'Alī.' This person appears to be the same as the Muḥib 'Alī who was the son of Mīr Khalīfah and was one of Akbar's trusted commanders (cf. Elliot, *History of India*, 5. 338; 6. 71–76).

Above this seal is written a memorandum (*A*) in Persian, 'Allāh Akbar (God is Most Great) — this was inspected (*'arḍ-dīdah shud*),[1] the day of Āsmān, 27th of the month presided over by Ardabahisht, of the Divine Reign, 24 (?) [*i.e.* in April, 1580 A.D. ?] at Lahore.'[2]

To the left of the same seal is another Persian memorandum (*B*), written in a different hand and running along the lower part of the page; it is a note describing the book as follows: 'Allāh Akbar (God is Most Great) — the Haft Paikar of Shaikh Niẓāmī, copied by Maulānā Aẓhar, containing seven [*sic*] pages of illuminated illustrations, the work of experts, for Mun'im Khān, the Khān-Khānān; 9000 single verses; five hundred rupees.'[3]

[1] As to the meaning of *'arḍ-dīdah*, see below, p. 112, note 1.

[2] There is some uncertainty as to the decipherment of the signs here read as '24,' located at a slight distance from the words for 'Divine Reign,' and somewhat below. If correctly deciphered, the year 24 appears to have been written, by an oversight, for 25 (a not unnatural slip to make, as the twenty-fifth year of the reign had begun but shortly before, and mistakes of a similar nature are to be found elsewhere, cf. Elliot, 5. 403, n. 1; 408, n. 1; 410, n. 1). The date (if the interpretation be correct) would correspond to April, 1580 A.D. (or the year when the manuscript was finally arranged), at which time Akbar was in the Panjāb, as we know from his chronicles, cf. Elliot, 5. 411 and 5. 246.

[3] <On the question of the identity of Maulānā Aẓhar, see above. The allusion to 'the work of experts' (*kār-i ūstādān*) refers alike to artist, copy-

The next memorandum in point of time, so far as can be judged, is the short Persian note (*C*) near the left-hand margin, above the large seal, which has been partly stamped over it. It reads: 'Allāh Akbar (God is Most Great) — this was inspected (*'arḍ-dīdah shud*) on the 13th of Ādar, year Alf [*i.e.* in March, 1582 A.D., reckoned according to Akbar's 'Era of the Thousand'; cf. Elliot, 5. 151, 159, n. 1, 534].'

The memorandum next in order (*D*), judging from the evidence, is the one immediately over seal 2, which is impressed somewhat higher than Akbar's signet, though by an official, on the right of the page. This seal (2), however, is only partially stamped, so that, except for the word *ikhlāṣ*, 'loyalty,' and some individual letters, the name can not be read; but even though it was certainly not Akbar's name, the seal must positively have been impressed in the latter part of his long reign, as shown by the date in the Persian note directly above it. This memorandum (*D*) reads: 'Allāh Akbar (God is Most Great) — it was inspected (*'arḍ-dīdah shud*) on the date, ninth of the month of Bahman, year 42 [*i.e.* about January, 1598].'

The last seal (3), the large one impressed on the left hand of the page, contains the name of Akbar's grandson, Shāh Jahān, combined with that of an official; it reads: 'Shāh Jahān — his servant I'timād Khān.' [1]

ist, gilder, illuminator, and possibly binder. The content of the memorandum indicates that the copy finally was especially arranged for Mun'im Khān as a gift to be presented to his sovereign.>

[1] The identity of the I'timād Khān named in this seal, is not certain. Two possible suggestions might be made. The first suggestion is that he may have been the same person as Sarmad I'timād Khān, an author and scholar, who was a devoted friend of Shāh Jahān's son Dārā and was put to death by Aurangzīb in 1660 A.D., after the execution of Dārā, as mentioned by Manucci, *Storia do Mogor*, transl. by Irvine, 1. 384, n. 1; 1.

The final memorandum (*E*), on the last page, is a note accompanying this latter seal and running in a narrow column between it and the colophon; it is written in a cursive Persian hand and reads as follows: 'On the 19th of Sha'bān, year 31 after the King's accession, [this book] was intrusted (*taḥwīl*) [1] to Khwājah Hilāl; 56 folios, 25 lines to each page, two couplets to a line; value 1300.' (This same figure is found also on the first page near the medallion.) This date (19th Sha'bān, year 31 of Shāh Jahān's reign) would correspond with May 22, 1658, or a month before Shāh Jahān was imprisoned by his son Aurangzīb (cf. Manucci, *Storia do Mogor*, 1. 294, n. 1).

A memorandum on the first page (fol. 1*a*) is simply a jotting in Persian to the effect that the work is 'the Haft Paikar of Niẓāmī, illustrated; 1300.' On the first of the fly-leaves which have been added at the front is likewise in Persian the title 'Haft Paikar' and a note that the copy 'passed to Jamajī Mobedī from Mīr Salmān Khān Sāmān.' On the top of the last folio is the signature of 'Chas Stuart Calcutta, March 24th, 1766'; and on the last of the fly-leaves added at the back, is written the name of 'Alex. Lord Blantyre.' There is an error in the pencil memorandum giving the date as 'A.H. 977' instead of 988, <but the statement, 'drawings by Baizad' (*sic*), in the same memorandum is in general correct, as now shown above.>

Subject and Contents. — The romantic story of Bahrām Gūr and the Seven Princesses, as described above.

223; and 4. 427, London, 1906. Another possibility would be to regard him as the same as I'timād ad-Daulah, whose full name was Muḥammad Amīn Khān and who enjoyed the favor both of Shāh Jahān and Aurangzīb down to the time prior to his death in 1721 A.D. (cf. Elliot, *History of India*, 7. 108–109, 442, 517).

[1] On the meaning of *taḥwīl*, see below, p. 112, n. 1.

Illuminations and Illustrations. — On the front page is a rich medallion in blue and gold with a dedicatory inscription to Akbar (as described above) in white letters. Then follows the opening of the poem on two richly illuminated full pages, with ornamental Kufic titles. There are likewise nine decorated small section-headings, ornately embellished, at different places in the poem, and there are numerous gold-lettered captions.

The painted miniatures are in the best style of the sixteenth century, recalling the characteristics of Bahzād's day. <They are, in fact, by Bahzād himself, as shown by his signatures, now noted on the miniatures, as mentioned above, after a re-examination of each painting since Mr. Martin's volume on miniatures appeared. They are painted after the Tīmūrid manner; but, as noted by Dr. W. R. Valentiner (*Bulletin of the Metropolitan Museum of Art*, 8. 80, no. 4, April, 1913), 'how much more delicate [than in Tīmūrid times] is the drawing of the figures, how much less crowded the composition, and how clearly Bahzād's treatment and remarkable sense of observation are shown in the details! The picture of Bahrām Gūr and the Indian Princess in the dark palace has exquisite rhythm of line; the hunting-scene shows the artist making clever use of large empty spaces in order to emphasize the most important figures, and is, moreover, remarkable for the characterization of the horses, which are vivid and lifelike in spite of their somewhat stiff attitude.' A Persian memorandum (already referred to) on the last page of the copy speaks of them as 'seven' in number and 'the work of experts'; it may now be added that Bahzād was the artist expert.> The original number of seven paintings has been reduced to five by the loss of folios 29 and 35. The subjects of the five miniatures in this noted manuscript illustrate incidents in the life of Bahrām Gūr, his fondness for hunting, and some of the stories told to him by the different princesses.

(*a*) fol. 1*a*. Illuminated medallion described above.

(*b*) fol. 1*b*. Illuminated full-page title with ornamental Kufic headings.

(*c*) fol. 2*a*. Second title-page similarly illuminated.

1 fol. 10*a*. Bahrām Gūr on the chase. (The fondness of Bahrām, 'that Great Hunter,' for the chase was proverbial.) <This miniature by Bahzād, signed in the lower right-hand corner, is now reproduced by Martin, 2. pl. 67*b*, right.>

2 fol. 17*b*. Bahrām Gūr's skill with the bow. (The familiar story of how Bahrām exhibited his skill to his sweetheart Fitnah, 'Mischief,' by transfixing with an arrow the hoof of a deer to its ear.) <Signed by Bahzād, lower left-hand corner.>

3 fol. 23*b*. Bahrām Gūr and the Indian Princess in the Dark Palace on Saturday. <Reproduced now by Martin, 2. pl. 67*a*, left, as signed by Bahzād. This signature is difficult to find, though the miniature is evidently Bahzād's work; a careful examination of the painting seems to reveal his name in minuscule letters in the lower left-hand corner of the pool, but the oxidation of the silver, which was used in painting the water, has made the writing almost illegible. Through an oversight Dr. Martin has wrongly entitled the subject of this illustration as 'Shīrīn.'>

4 fol. 33*b*. How a hunter was drowned in a well. (To illustrate the story told to Bahrām about the hunter drowned in a well that was covered with an earthen jar so as to decoy animals that came to drink. A wayfarer uses the branch of a tree in trying to find the missing man's body.) <Signed near lower right-hand corner by Bahzād.>

5 fol. 47*a*. The eavesdropper. (Illustration of the story told to Bahrām of the fate of the eavesdropper who

peeped from the lattice window. The eavesdropper is represented in the picture, and above the lattices is an arabesque inscription containing praises of the King, and along the cornice runs an Arabic couplet, 'God is without equal, and Him alone we will worship.' Over the doorway in a conventionalized Kufic is, 'O Thou Opener of the Door [*i.e.* God]!') <Signed in the lower right corner by Bahzād.>

11

A Persian Anthology — Niẓāmī abridged; Selections also from other well-known Persian Writers. — An early nineteenth century illuminated manuscript containing the five poetical works of Niẓāmī in an abridged form, and selections from thirty or forty works by other writers, mostly poets, including Firdausī, Farīd ad-Dīn 'Aṭṭār, 'Umar Khayyām (?), Sa'dī, Jalāl ad-Dīn Rūmī, Ḥāfiẓ, Jāmī, and others. The selections are handsomely written on the margins as well as in the body of the manuscript, the entire compilation having been made at one and the same time. The copy is illuminated by sixteen full-page miniatures and five marginal paintings; all being in the style of the period.

Size. — 10½ × 7 in. (26.5 × 17.7 cm.); written surface, 9¾ × 6 in. (24.7 × 15.3 cm.). Folios 163. A number of folios are missing; there are lacunae, for example, after 25*b*, 48*b*, 106*b*, 108*b*, 109*b*, 112*b*, 116*b*, 120*b*. The manuscript breaks off abruptly, and the last page is left blank, as if the copyist had been interrupted in the midst of his work.

Binding. — Black leather Oriental binding (not original) with gold ornamentation on the outside and with reddish leather on the inside.

Writing and Paper. — Small, clear Nasta'līq in a fair hand; 27 lines to a page in five gold-ruled columns; the prose selections are likewise written 27 lines to the page. The writing in the case of the marginal selections is slightly smaller, but is by the same hand throughout as the body of the text. The paper is of a good quality with a slight ivory gloss. The side margins of all the pages had become worn by usage and have been skilfully repaired throughout.

Date and Scribe. — Despite its much-used appearance, which gives to the manuscript the semblance of being older than it is, the copy must belong to the first part of the nineteenth century, if we may judge by the date 123[0] A.H. = 1815 A.D., recorded by the scribe on two different pages. First on fol. 117*b* (margin), at the end of the selections from Sa'dī's *Būstān*, there is a memorandum by the copyist, written in black ink, overscored with red, as follows: 'Here end the selections from the Būstān of Shaikh Sa'dī (upon whom be mercy!); dated, month of Rajab, in the year 123[0] A.H. [= June, 1815 A.D.]; written at the command of his lordship Āqā Ḥusain (whom God protect!).' Second, on fol. 127*b* (in the body of the text, and written a month earlier than the marginal note just described) there is a similar memorandum, but by a different hand and in a cursive style that is difficult to decipher; it occurs in a panel following the *Ghazals* of Salmān of Sāwah, and is written in red ink; the substance is as follows: 'At the command of his lordship . . . Āqā Muḥammad Ḥusain (whom God protect!) and with his support and suggestion as to some of the marginal selections, this book was prepared (?) by me, Qāḍī Aḥmad [. . .], the student, in hopes that when it comes to his glorious presence, it may meet with the acceptance of that dignitary; dated Jumāda II, 123[0] A.H. [= May, 1815].' Although the memorandum is difficult to decipher and the sense is not clear in every detail, the import of the passage is plain, namely, that the scribe (Aḥmad . . .) had received suggestions from his patron in regard to some of the selections chosen to be copied. It may be inferred, furthermore, from the dedication in the vignettes on the title-pages that this patron designed the manuscript as a gift to the Persian grandee whose name is there duly mentioned. Simply by way of record it may be added that there is no special bearing on the date of this manuscript in the colophon that concludes the selections from Salmān himself (fol. 127*b*), 'Jumāda I, 814 A.H. [= August, 1411 A.D.],' because that colophon is merely a verbatim reproduction of an older colophon, even including the name of the earlier scribe, 'Maḥmūd Murtaḍā al-Ḥusainī.'

Dedication. — The two large circular medallions on the illuminated title-pages of the manuscript show that the book was personally dedicated by its donor to an Ottoman merchant prince, if we may so localize the attribute 'Rūmī' in his title. The inscriptions in these dedicatory medallions read respectively as follows: (1) 'The owner, and whatever is his, belongs to God. The honorable Khwājah, prince of merchants of the world.' (2) 'Kamāl ad-Dīn Maḥmūd . . . [*lacuna*] Rūmī (may God grant him peace!).' From what has been noted above we may presume that the book was presented to this gentleman, who was a man of culture as well as a man of business.

Memorandums. — On the front fly-leaf is a memorandum in Armenian, 'M 63/16th,' evidently the number of the manuscript in a book-list; there are also two pencil notes of no importance. On fol. 1*a* there is an Arabic quotation and one in Persian. The Arabic citation is Qur'ānic, from the chapter entitled Ṣūrat al-A'rāf (7. 55) as follows: 'Verily your Lord is God, He who created the heavens and the earth in six days. He then ascended to His throne. He causeth the night to cover the day — it succeedeth it swiftly. He created likewise the sun and the moon and the stars, which are subject to his command. Is not creation and its command His! Blessed be God, the Lord of the Worlds!'

The Persian quotation on this page gives the name of a former owner of the book and cites a verse of a personal nature: 'In the words of the owner, a Sayyid, the Sayyid Āqā Ja'far — may God's mercy be upon him!

'Let three of the four seasons be thine, and spring alone be mine;
Let the face of the whole earth be thine — but let union with the Beloved be mine.'

There is a further jotting on this fly-leaf in Persian with regard to the title and contents, 'Makhzan al-Asrār of Niẓāmī and two other books,' but this statement is both incomplete and inadequate, as shown below.

On the back of the last fly-leaf there is penciled a note in English: 'Niẓāmī's Khamsah, etc.,' together with a memorandum in ink, '12 large and 5 small miniatures.' Either there was an error in this statement or the manuscript has lost a miniature since the memorandum was made, as the copy at present contains 11 (not 12) large and 5 small miniatures.

Subject and Arrangement. — The contents of the manuscript are miscellaneous, as is shown by the Persian title-pages, even though not every title there given appears to be represented in the copy in its present form; and some of the selections that do occur appear to be missing in the title list. More than half of the body of the work is devoted to selections from Niẓāmī. Specimens also are given from Firdausī, Sa'dī, Ḥāfiẓ, and other writers, the passages in the margins sometimes being from the same author as in the body of the text. In the list of authors mentioned on the first illuminated page is the name of 'Umar Khayyām. No special section is assigned to him in the manuscript, but it may be remotely possible that the fifteen Rubā'īs on the margin of fol. 126*b*–127*a* are wandering quatrains of his, as they resemble his verses in tone; but it has not been possible thus far to identify these stanzas with any of those generally ascribed to 'Umar. For the sake merely of comparison and reference a record is here made of the imperfect list of authors (*fihrist*) as it is given in the illuminated circles placed around the two medallions on the first two title-pages; but it must be remembered that in a number of instances this table does *not* agree with the actual contents of the manuscript; the names of Ḥāfiẓ and Sa'dī, for instance, are not included in the list, although a section of the volume is actually devoted to selections from their works.

I. *First page list of titles.*
  1. Book of Fragments of Ibn-i Yamīn.
  2. Book of *Rubā'īs* of 'Umar Khayyām.
  3. Book of the great Maulānā 'Abd ar-Raḥmān Jāmī.
  4. Book of Darvīsh Ḥasan Qalandar [latter half of the sixteenth century — see Ethé, *Grundriss*, 2. 359].

II. *Second page list of titles.*
  1. Selections from the *Khamsah* of Niẓāmī.
  2. A book on the science of chemistry.
  3. A book on perforating crown pearls [*i.e.* on writing poetry].
  4. Selections from the *Tawārīkh-i Niẓām*, on poetic dates.
  5. A book on medical subjects.
  6. Selections from the *Natā'ij al-Afkār*, or about the results of taking thought.
  7. *Ghazals*, or odes.
  8. *Qaṣīdahs*, or panegyrics in verse.
  9. Selections from 'Aṭṭār's *Manṭiq aṭ-Ṭair*, or 'Language of Birds.'
  10. Artificial and unartificial *Qaṣīdahs*.
  11. Selections from Firdausī's *Shāh-nāmah*. [They relate to Rūm, or Byzantium.]
  12. *Tarjī'āt*, poems with refrains.

13. Selections from Rūmī's *Maṣnawī.*
14. Miscellaneous *Qaṣīdahs* of adjuration.
15. Selections from Sanā'ī's *Ḥadīqah,* or 'Garden.'
16. Poems of advice and admonition.
17. Nāṣir Khusrau's *Raushanā'ī-nāmah.*
18. A book on stringing pearls [*i.e.* on writing poetry].
19. The book of *Niṣāb aṣ-Ṣibiān.*
20. Introduction to astrological poetry.
21. The book of *Abkār al-Afkār*, or 'Maiden Thoughts.'
22. Ten treatises by Auhadī of Kirmān.
23. About the oneness of God the Most High.
24. In praise of the Prophet and his incomparableness.

A. Texts in the body of the book.

fol. 2*b*–13*a*. A portion of Niẓāmī's *Makhzan al-Asrār.*

fol. 13*b*–34*a*. A selection from Niẓāmī's *Khusrau and Shīrīn.*

fol. 34*b*–48*b*. From Niẓāmī's *Lailā and Majnūn.* [Several pages are missing at the end owing to a lacuna in the manuscript.]

fol. 49*a*–64*a*. Selections from Niẓāmī's *Haft Paikar.*

fol. 64*b*–81*a*. From the First portion (*a*) of Niẓāmī's *Book of Alexander*, here entitled *Sharaf-nāmah.*

fol. 81*b*–95*b*. From the Second portion (*b*) of Niẓāmī's *Book of Alexander*, here entitled *Iskandar-nāmah*, though more often called *Khirad-nāmah.*

fol. 95*b*–102*a*. From Firdausī's *Shāh-nāmah.* [The selections relate to King Gushtāsp and the Princess of Rūm; cf. ed. Vullers and Landauer, 3. 1451–1496.]

fol. 102*a*–103*a*. Selections from Sa'dī.

fol. 103*b*–106*b*. Selected *Qaṣīdahs* in praise of the unity of God by various authors (Fakhr ad-Dīn 'Irāqī, Anwarī, Sarāj ad-Dīn Qamarī, Adīb Ṣābir, 'Abd al-Qādir of Nā'īn, Sayyid Jalāl 'Aḍūd, Shaikh Sa'dī.

fol. 107*a*–113*a*. *Ghazals* of Maulānā Salmān of Sāwah (*c.* 1300–1376 A.D.; cf. Muqtadir, *Cat. Pers. Mss. at Bankipore*, vol. 1. p. 219–227).

fol. 113*b*–118*b*. *Ghazals* of Ḥāfiẓ.

fol. 118*b*–121*b*. *Ghazals* of Muḥammad Shīrīn Maghribī of Nā'īn (d. 1406 A.D. — see Rieu, *Cat. Pers. Mss. British Museum* 2. 633 and *Supplement*, p. 181;

Ethé, *Neupers. Litt.*, p. 304; Muqtadir, *Cat. Pers.*, vol. 2. p. 6–9).

fol. 121*b*–123*b*. *Qaṣīdahs* and *Tarjī'āt* of Saif ad-Dīn Isfrangī (d. 1267 or 1268 A.D.).

fol. 124*a*–127*b*. A collection of artificial acrostic verses by Salmān of Sāwah (*c.* 1300–1376 A.D., see above), whose name appears in the head-band (fol. 124*b*), one page after the beginning. [In these selections the syllables of the words that contain artificial devices are indicated by red ink in contrast to the black ink; and red ink is used in the marginal columns to give the precise name of each meter that is involved in the versification.]

fol. 128*b*–134*b*. The *Lama'āt* of 'Irāqī of Hamadān (d. 1287 or 1289 A.D., see Rieu, *Cat. Pers. Mss. Brit. Mus.*, 2. 594). — [A treatise in verse and prose on mystic love.]

fol. 135*a*–136*b*. 'Irāqī's mystic work headed by the phrase as title 'Allah is the Lord of Success' — [mainly in prose].

fol. 137*a*–154*a*. 'Irāqī's mystic work headed by the titular phrase 'God of Assistance and Guidance'— [mainly in prose].

fol. 154*b*–156*b*. Prose selections containing mystic speculations, or the *Ā'īn al-Quḍāt* of Abu'l Ma'ālī 'Abdallah b. Muḥammad b. 'Alī al-Miyānjī, a native of Miyānah, east of Lake Urumiah, and a mystic writer, who died in 1130 or 1138 A.D. (cf. Rieu, *op. cit.*, 1. 411).

fol. 157*a*–163*a*. From the first part of Sa'dī's *Gulistān*. [This is broken off abruptly in the middle of a sentence at the beginning of Anecdote 28; the last page of the manuscript is left blank, as if the copyist had been interrupted in his work.]

B. Text on the margins of the book.

fol. 2*b*–38*a*. Farīd ad-Dīn 'Aṭṭār's *Manṭiq aṭ-Ṭair* (practically complete).

fol. 38*b*–58*a*. From Jalāl ad-Dīn Rūmī's *Maṣnawī*.

fol. 58*b*–65*b*. From Nāṣir Khusrau's *Raushanā'ī* (cf. Browne, *Lit. Hist. of Persia*, 2. 221, 244–246). [It may be noted that on fol. 65*b* (on the side margin) near the close of the selections there is given the date 343 A.H. (= 954–955 A.D.), which thus agrees with the date in the Leyden manuscript and two Paris manuscripts as opposed to the other noted by Browne, *Lit. Hist.*, 2. 244–245.]

fol. 66*a*–75*a*. A discourse in verse upon prayer and ceremonial observances by Mullā Sharaf ad-Dīn Bukhārī (1303 A.D.; cf. Ethé, *Neupersische Litteratur*, p. 309).

fol. 75*b*–88*a*. A versified composition entitled *Abkār al-Afkār*, 'Maiden Thoughts,' being stories about feminine ornaments and maiden meditations.

fol. 88*b*–97*a*. Ten letters in verse by Rukn ad-Dīn Auḥadī of Marāgha and Isfahān, who died about 738 A.H. = 1337 A.D. (See Rieu, 2. 619; and Muqtadir, 1. 200–202.)

fol. 97*b*–102*b*. From Sa'dī's *Būstān*.

fol. 103*a*. From Jāmī.

fol. 103*b*–105*a*. *Ghazals*, or odes, by various authors (Khāqānī, Firdausī, Sarāj ad-Dīn of Balkh, Farīd ad-Dīn al-Aḥūl, Farīd ad-Dīn 'Aṭṭār, Aṣīr ad-Dīn Akhsīkatī, Shaikh Sa'dī, Fakhr ad-Dīn Ra'īs Maḥmūd, Rafī' ad-Dīn Abharī, Maulānā Sharaf ad-Dīn, Maulānā Sarāj ad-Dīn Qamarī, from the Shāh-nāmah, Khāqānī [repeated], Sayyid Ḥasan Ghaznavī, Farīd ad-Dīn 'Aṭṭār [repeated], Afḍal ad-Dīn Kirmānī).

fol. 105*a*–106*b*. Selection from Jāmī's *Yūsuf and Zulaikhā*, describing how Joseph is carried captive to Egypt and is seen by Potiphar's wife. [A lacuna follows, see remark as to fol. 118*a* below.]

fol. 107*a*–117*b*. From Sa'dī's *Būstān* (a selection of thirty-six stories).

fol. 118*a*–124*a* top. From Jāmī's *Yūsuf and Zulaikhā*. [The story of Joseph is abruptly resumed, some pages having presumably been lost.]

fol. 124*a*–125*a* top. A composition in verse called *Nān u Halwā*, or 'Bread and Sweetmeats' (relating to ascetic life, by Shaikh Bahā'ī, who died in 1620 or 1621 A.D.).

fol. 125*a* top–126*b* bottom. *Natā'ij al-Afkār*, or 'Reflections,' in ghazal form.

fol. 126*b* bottom–127*a* top. Fifteen *Rubā'īs*, or Quatrains. [No author is named in direct connection with these quatrains, although 'Umar Khayyām's name appears in the list of authors on the first title-page of the manuscript; but thus far, as noted above, it has not been possible to identify any of these quatrains with those in received editions of his verses.]

fol. 127*b*. From the *Sāqī-nāmah* of Mashriqī (cf. Rieu, p. 682*a*, 683*a*.)

fol. 128*a*. A selection from Jāmī.

fol. 128*b*–133*a*. Prose selections from 'Irāqī's *'Ushshāq-nāmah*. [These supplement in a manner the selections from the same author in the body of the text and are headed by the words 'Praise and Gratitude to God.']

fol. 133*a*–136*a*. Verses and prose passages on 'Admonition' by 'Irāqī. [In the decorative marginal title-band are the words: 'Praise be to the Lord of Praise.' The first sixteen lines of the text are in Arabic; the rest that follows is in Persian.]

fol. 136*a*–144*a*. Verses and prose passages on 'Admonition' continued. [In the decorative title-band are the words: 'In the Name of God; we desire His Praise!']

fol. 144*b*–163*a*. Prose selections relating to theological and spiritual matters. [In the decorated marginal band is simply the heading: 'I triumph in the Praise of God.']

Illuminations and Illustrations. — The two illuminated title-pages, with a series of names of authors and words ornately introduced into small circles around the central inscribed vignettes, have been mentioned above. Throughout the work there are ornamental panel headings as introductions to the principal selections or paragraphs, and similarly rhomb-shaped bands are let into the margins to indicate the various sections; there are likewise decorative flower designs on the margins, and gold is freely used throughout as an added embellishment.

There are 16 full-page miniatures and 5 marginal miniatures, the marginal paintings being employed to illustrate the material that occurs in the marginal texts. All the miniatures are the work of a single artist under the Bukhāran influence, and in style they seem to represent the art of Persia in the first part of the nineteenth century, to which the manuscript belongs. The more specific details as to the illuminations here follow.

I (*a*) fol. 1*b*–2*a*. Illuminated title-pages.

(*b*) fol. 2*b*–3*a*. Illuminated title-pages of Niẓāmī's *Makhzan al-Asrār*, or 'Treasury of Mysteries.'

1 fol. 4*b* (full page). Ascension of Muḥammad to heaven in a vision. (Illustrating Niẓāmī's *Makhzan al-Asrār.*)

2 fol. 11*a* (margin). Shaikh San'ān falls in love with a Christian girl. (Illustration of Farīd ad-Dīn 'Aṭṭār's story — cf. Browne, *Lit. Hist.*, 2. 513.)

3 fol. 13*a* (margin). Shaikh San'ān and his Christian sweet-heart united.

II (*c*) fol. 13*b*. Decorative head-band to Niẓāmī's *Khusrau and Shīrīn.*

4 fol. 19*b* (full page). King Khusrau riding out on his horse Shabdīz, 'Black-as-night.'

5 fol. 24*b* (full). Shīrīn goes to see the sculptured work of Farhād, her artist-lover.

6 fol. 30*b* (margin). The dervish who was to be hanged for

love of his prince dies when he beholds him. (Illustrating 'Aṭṭār's *Manṭiq aṭ-Ṭair*, ch. 44, cf. Garcin de Tassy, p. 224–229.)

III (*d*) fol. 34*b*. Decorative head-band to Niẓāmī's *Lailā and Majnūn.*

7 fol. 40*b* (full). Combat between Majnūn's friend Naufal and the tribe of Lailā.

8 fol. 44*b* (margin). Muḥammad and 'Alī.

IV [(*e*)] [No title-heading has been preserved for Niẓāmī's story of Bahrām Gūr, owing to the loss of several folios in the manuscript, as noted above.]

9 fol. 50*b* (full). Bahrām Gūr and his sweetheart Fitnah (both in the upper part of the picture). (Illustrating the well-known story of Bahrām Gūr, told by Niẓāmī as well as by Firdausī, on 'practice makes perfect.')

10 fol. 52*a* (full). Bahrām Gūr and the Princess in the Red Palace. (Illustrating Niẓāmī's romance of Bahrām Gūr.)

11 fol. 56*a* (full). The man drowned in the well. (Illustrating Niẓāmī's story alluded to above (p. 78), under manuscript 10, fol. 33*b*.)

V (*f*) fol. 64*b*. Illuminated head-band to Niẓāmī's first division of the *Book of Alexander*, here called *Sharaf-nāmah.*

(*g*) fol. 81*b*. Illuminated head-band to the second division, which here, however, bears the title *Kitāb-i Iskandar-nāmah.*

12 fol. 85*b* (margin). A convivial scene between two young men. (Illustrating the treatise called 'Maiden Thoughts,' which is written on the margin.)

13 fol. 91*b* (full). Alexander in India sees some maidens in swimming. (Illustration of a passage in Niẓāmī's *Book of Alexander*, second part.)

VI (*h*) fol. 95*b*. Decorative head-band to selection from Firdausī's *Shāh-nāmah.*

14 fol. 99*b* (full). Gushtāsp plays polo with the Emperor of Rūm, with whose daughter he has fallen in love.

(To illustrate a passage in the selection from the *Shāh-nāmah*.)

15 fol. 102*b* (full). An equestrian scene. (To illustrate a selection from Sa'dī.)

VII (*i*) fol. 103*b*. Head-band to *Qaṣīdahs* by various authors.

VIII (*j*) fol. 107*a*. Decorative head-band to the Ghazals of Salmān of Sāwah.

16 fol. 128*a* (full). A king enjoying music and wine. (To illustrate a reference by Jāmī in the marginal text.)

IX (*k*) fol. 128*b*. Decorative head-band for 'Irāqī's *Lama'āt*.

(*l*) fol. 135*a*. Illuminated title-panel—'God is the Lord of success.'

(*m*) fol. 137*a*. Illuminated title-panel — 'God is the Lord of success.'

(*n*) fol. 154*b*. Illuminated introductory panel in Kufic.

X (*o*) fol. 157*a*. Introductory head-band to Sa'dī's *Gulistān*, but not inscribed.

III

JALĀL AD-DĪN RŪMĪ

JALĀL AD-DĪN RŪMĪ

(1207–1273 A.D.)

Jalāl ad-Dīn Rūmī, the most renowned of the Persian philosopher-poets and one of the greatest of Eastern mystics, was born September 30, 1207 A.D., in Balkh, an ancient city still existing in Northern Afghānistān.

Trained by his father, Bahā ad-Dīn, a noted teacher who was descended from a noble family, Jalāl became imbued, from the outset, with the Ṣūfī doctrines of Divine Love and spiritual longing for union of the soul with the Supreme Being. His father's mystic teachings and preaching, however, aroused the opposition of the ruling monarch at the time; as a consequence, parent and son, the latter still a small boy, were obliged to leave Balkh.

Accompanying his father, the lad journeyed westward, visiting Mecca and making various sojourns at other places, until after a number of years they both found royal protection and patronage at Iconium (Qūniah) in Rūm, or Asia Minor, the name Rūm being applied to that portion of the Byzantine Empire of Rome. From his long residence in this territory he received the appellation *Rūmī*, 'the Rūmian, or Roman.'

On the death of his father, in 1231 A.D., he succeeded to the headship of the collegiate institution at Iconium, which the latter had held. Much, therefore, is known regarding Rūmī's personal history, his family life, and the career which raised him to high renown as a mystic philosopher, poetic teacher, and religious devotee, down to the time of his death on Sunday, December 17, 1273 A.D.

The fact that Jalāl ad-Dīn Rūmī was the founder of the Maulawī sect of 'whirling, or dancing, dervishes,' so called, will always be associated with his name, and for that reason he is perhaps most often designated by the title Maulānā, 'Our Lord,' *i.e.* of the Monastic Order. The establishment of this noted sect was made in commemoration of the death of a wandering dervish, Shams ad-Dīn of Tabrīz, in 1246 A.D., under the strong influence of whose esoteric teachings Rūmī had come three years before, and largely in honor of whose memory he also composed a series of lyric poems, highly spiritual in tone, afterwards collected into a *Dīwān*.

Rūmī's lasting poetic fame, however, rests on the *Maṣnawī*, a work of about 30,000 couplets, in six books, teaching moral philosophy and mysticism under the guise of an allegorical interpretation of verses in the Qur'ān, and through the medium of anecdotes, precepts, parables, and legends, esoteric in meaning. This work complete is contained in the manuscript described below.

For abundant biographical and bibliographical material regarding Rūmī see H. Ethé, *Neupersische Litteratur*, in Geiger and Kuhn's *Grundriss*, 2. 289–291; P. Horn, *Geschichte der persischen Litteratur*, p. 161–168; and E. G. Browne, *Literary History of Persia*, 2. 515–525. In regard to the Maṣnawī, reference may be made to an abridged translation into English by E. H. Whinfield, *Mathnawī*, London, 1898, which is a standard work; and to a partial rendering into German by G. Rosen, *Mesnevī*, Leipzig, 1849. The first book of the Maṣnawī has been turned into English also by J. W. Redhouse, 1881; and the second book has been admirably translated and commented on in two volumes by C. E. Wilson, *The Maṣnavī, Book II*, London, 1910 (Probsthain & Co.). For the Dīwān consult also R. A. Nicholson, *Selected Odes from the Dīwān*, Cambridge, 1898; W. Hastie, London, 1903; and compare F. H. Davis, *Persian Mystics*, London, 1907.

12

Rūmī: Maṣnawī, complete in six books. The manuscript belongs to the last quarter of the fifteenth century, being dated in 1489 A.D.; it is handsomely illuminated, besides being illustrated by four full-page miniature paintings.

Size. — $11\frac{1}{8} \times 7\frac{1}{2}$ in. (28.5 × 19.0 cm.); written surface, $7\frac{3}{4} \times 4\frac{5}{8}$ in. (19.6 × 12.0 cm.). Folios 355. One folio is missing at the end of the third book, before fol. 172, and one is lost at the beginning of the sixth book, before fol. 297.

Binding. — Original Oriental binding in a golden brown leather. The outside covers have a blind-pressed rectangular field gracefully decorated with tendril traceries, and slightly dusted with gold; the whole is then surrounded with panels, stamped with a floweret design, and bound by a double gilt cording. The inside covers are of maroon leather with an elongated medallion and corner angles of perforated gilt work upon a light bluish background; the field is framed by a gilt cording.

Writing and Paper. — Written in good clear Nasta'līq of medium size, 20 lines to a page in four columns, outlined by rulings of green, orange, gold, and blue. There are a great number of rubrics giving the title, or subject, of the many poetic themes. The paper is of medium weight and is strong in texture; it has a *café au lait* tinge and shows a slight sheen.

Date and Scribe. — The date is given three times in the manuscript in figures as 894 A.H. = 1488–1489 A.D., first at the end of the first book (fol. 58*a*), then at the end of the second book (fol. 108*a*), and finally in the colophon. The copying was therefore completed in one year, but no months are mentioned. The scribe does not give his name.

Memorandums. — On the front fly-leaf, at the upper left-hand corner, is a stock number written in Persian, and a kindred annotation in English figures. On the back of the first folio is a Persian memorandum, but it is partly defaced and can not be deciphered with the exception of a date, 'year 1193 A.H. [= 1779 A.D.].' On the top of this page, toward the left-hand corner, is an impression of an oval seal, but it is not legible.

On the last page of the text (fol. 355*b*), to the right of the colophon, is a Persian inscription that reads: 'In the year 1259 A.H., in the month of Ṣafar [= March, 1843], at the time when (I was) in the city of Khamsah [in a district in northwestern Persia] this book of Maulawī [*i.e.* Rūmī] (may God have mercy upon him!) was received by the humble servant as a present from his lordship, the noble prince and vicegerent Mahdī Qulī Mīrzā (may his glory and rule be everlasting!).' Directly following this, and still to the right of the colophon, is another memorandum, partly obliterated, but the close of it can be made out as follows: 'The Pādishāh Muḥammad Shāh, whose justice is like that of Jām, in the month of Rabī' awwal, 1260 A.H. [= March, 1844].' The reference is evidently to Muḥammad Shāh, of Persia, who was ruling at that time. A memorandum to the left of the colophon has been effaced, and some seals and a short notation have been similarly obliterated.

On the back of the last fly-leaf are two memorandums in Persian; the longer one reads, with repetitions, as follows: 'Hūwa [*i.e.* God] is the Lord whose aid is besought. The date of the birth of the Light of the Eyes, Mīrzā Ḥasan 'Alī (may the Lord of the World protect and bless his birth!) was the nineteenth of the month of Muḥarram, on Monday, 19th of the month of Muḥarram, 1264 A.H. [= Dec. 27, 1847].' The shorter memorandum, just above it, reads: 'The birth of the Light of the Eyes, Nūshābah, was in the month of Ṣafar, 1265 A.H. [= January, 1849]. May God bless the birth!'

Throughout the codex there are numerous marginal annotations, which may be classified as follows: (1) variant readings from other manuscripts; (2) certain additional couplets taken from another copy or copies with which this manuscript has been compared; (3) explanations of certain difficult or archaic words.

Subject and Arrangement. — The Maṣnawī of Rūmī in about 28,000 couplets; the manuscript is divided into six books (*daftars*), each introduced by a separate 'unwān, or illuminated title-piece. — I. The first book, beginning with a single page of prose preface in Arabic, occupies fol. 1*b*–58*a*. — II. The second book opens with a page of prose preface in Persian, and occupies fol. 58*b*–108*a*. — III. The third book, without a preface, comprises fol. 108*b*–172*a*. — IV. The fourth book, without preface, covers fol. 172*b*–234*a*. — V. The fifth book, with two pages of prose preface in Arabic and Persian, occupies fol. 234*b*–296*b*. — VI. The sixth book comprises fol. 297*a*–355*b*.

Illuminations and Illustrations. — The manuscript has five 'unwāns, or title-pieces, of rich design and soft coloring. The two opening pages, moreover, of Books I, II, and III are heightened by heavy gold interlineations with orange, blue, and yellow studdings. Reference has already been made to the frequent rubric headings in the text. The margins around the four miniatures are highly embellished. These paintings appear to be the work of two different artists. The two frontispiece scenes of the chase and the fine miniatures on fol. 296*b*, with ornate borders of blue illumination, may be from a single brush. On the other hand, the miniature on fol. 172*a*, with its heavy gold background and gilded margin, appears to be by a different hand. All four, however, recall the style of the later Tīmūrid period. <Now, since the appearance of Martin's

book, it may be added that the exceptional miniature on fol. 172*a* closely resembles in certain details, especially in the drawing of the plane tree and the lineaments of the bearded elderly man, two paintings by Bahzād (Martin, 2. pl. 75*b*, 74*a*; cf. 1. 44) in a manuscript dated 1485 A.D., or three years earlier than the present codex, which bears the date 1488–1489 A.D.>

The main points regarding the illuminations and illustrations are as follows: —

1–2 fol. 1*b*–2*a*. Two frontispiece miniatures representing scenes from the chase.

I (*a*) fol. 2*b*. Illuminated ‘unwān, or title-piece, to Book One. This page and fol. 3*a* have also the gold interlineation between the verses, as described above.

II (*b*) fol. 58*b*. Illuminated title-piece to Book Two, with gold interlineation on this and the following page.

III (*c*) fol. 108*b*. Illuminated title-piece to Book Three, with similar gold interlineations on both pages.

3 fol. 172*a*. Miniature painting of two persons listening to readings by two poets to the accompaniment of music. [Possibly the gray-bearded man may represent Rūmī, and the person seated on his left may, perhaps, be Ḥasan Ḥusam ad-Dīn, his favorite pupil and amanuensis.] <For a comment on this miniature, see above, p. 97–98.>

IV (*d*) fol. 172*b*. Illuminated title-piece to Book Four.

V (*e*) fol. 234*b*. Illuminated title-piece to Book Five.

4 fol. 296*b*. Miniature of a youthful king seated upon a pavilion throne on a terrace overlooking a garden, and served by two attendants.

VI [(*f*)] [The ‘unwān to Book Six is missing, owing to the loss of a leaf between folios 296 and 297.]

IV

SA'DĪ

SA'DĪ

(1184–1291 A.D.)

Sa'dī, poet and moralist, and generally conceded to be the most popular writer in Persian literature, was born about the year 1184 A.D. in Shīrāz, Southern Persia, where his father appears to have held an official position under the Atābek rulers of Fārs. After his father's death he received educational aid for a long time from the Atābek prince, Sa'd bin Zangī, in honor of whom he assumed the literary name Sa'dī by which he is known to fame. This patronage enabled the young man to study at Baghdād until 1226 A.D., and among his teachers was the eminent Shams ad-Dīn Abu'l Faraj ibn al-Jauzī, whose portrait with the youthful Sa'dī is depicted in the first miniature in manuscript No. 13, described below.

For the next thirty years of his life, or from 1226 to 1256, he traveled as a dervish pilgrim through many lands, visiting Northeastern Īrān, India, Arabia, Abyssinia, Syria, Northern Africa, and Asia Minor.

In 1256, when over seventy years of age, he returned to his native city and devoted the rest of his long life to the literary pursuits which he had begun in his early days. In the next year he had finished his poetic work, the *Būstān,* in ten cantos of verse, and in the following twelvemonth, 1258, he had completed his still more famous *Gulistān,* a Persian classic in prose and verse, upon which his greatest renown rests, especially as an ethical teacher. He was the author likewise of a large number of lyric and miscellaneous compositions, as is shown by the contents of the manuscript No. 13, described below, which contains his works complete, except the *Pand-nāmah,* the authenticity of which is doubtful. Sa'dī's death occurred in 1291 A.D.

For further details regarding Sa'dī's life and works, consult Browne, *Literary History of Persia,* 2. 525–539; Ethé, *Neupersische Litteratur,* p. 292–296; Horn, *Geschichte der persischen Litteratur,* p. 168–175; and compare Jackson, *Persia Past and Present,* p. 333–335.

13

Sa'dī: Kulliyyāt, or works complete. This large manuscript contains the collected works of Sa'dī, and belongs apparently to about the middle of the sixteenth century. It is embellished by a full-page illuminated frontispiece and numerous half-page title-pieces, besides other ornamentations; and it is illustrated by twelve miniatures, two of these preceding the frontispiece as full-page paintings, and two of them, likewise full-page, following the close of the book. All the miniatures except the first one are from the brush of a single artist, who remains anonymous.

Size. — 16¼ × 8½ in. (41.5 × 21.5 cm.); written surface, 9⅞ × 5 in. (25.2 × 13.0 cm.). Folios 480. There are missing three folios — one each between folios 99–100, 140–141, 474–475 — but otherwise the codex seems to be complete, even though a few catchwords have been accidentally omitted. A Persian memorandum on the back of the last folio, four times repeated in words and in figures by two different hands, gives the number as 'four hundred and eighty-seven folios' or '487 folios'; but, as the pages were not numbered, the count may not have been quite exact, as such mistakes have been found in Persian countings in other manuscripts that are complete.

Binding. — Persian binding of black leather with blind-pressed designs in gilt. These gilded patterns on the exterior of the covers comprise a large oblong medallion with double pendants above and below; the corner angles harmonize in style, and there is a running flowered border of gilt to frame the field. On each of the two small oval pendants directly above and below the central medallion of both outer covers, and thus four times repeated, is tooled in raised Persian letters: 'The work (*'amal*) of Ḥasan ibn

Recitation of Poems to the Accompaniment of Music
Ms. No. 12, fol. 172*a* (see page 98)

al-Ḥusainī Muḥammad.' This seems to refer to the name of the binder who executed the work; but if another interpretation should be given, namely that it referred to the calligraphist who copied the work, the conjecture might be made that it was the famous penman Ḥasan ibn Muḥammad, of Larissa, who transcribed a manuscript in 1611 A.D. (= 1020 A.H.), according to Huart, *Les Calligraphes et les miniaturistes*, p. 263.

The interior of the covers is of a dark tan leather without gilding or color, but ornamented with blind-pressed corner angles and a central medallion offset by four pendants that form a cross.

The pages have not been trimmed, but the folios have been remounted when the binding was repaired; the repairing may account for the loss of the three missing folios.

Writing and Paper. — The writing is in a good bold Nasta'līq hand. The prose portions are written in a single broad column and in a narrower marginal column; the verse portions, in a double column and in a marginal column of the same size as before. The body columns run 16 lines to a page; the marginal columns run 12 lines to a page. Broad gold rules divide the columns, and heavy outlines in colors frame the written part of the page, the whole being then enclosed by a thin double ruling of black near the edge. There are numerous words written in rubrics in the Preface and in the *Gulistān*. The paper is of a rather heavy quality with an ivory finish and runs fairly even. The first two folios with double illuminations and paintings are of an extra heavy paper.

Date and Scribe. — The manuscript gives neither the name of the scribe nor the date, but, judging from the style of the miniatures and illuminations, it belongs approximately to the middle of the sixteenth century. Compare also the possibility referred to above, under 'Binding.' The quality of the scribe's handwriting has already been mentioned.

Memorandums. — There are memorandums on the margins of a half dozen or more folios, but they are not of special importance — for example, a chance jotting on fol. 410*a* 'Jahāngīr Khān 'Ālamgīr'; on fol. 217*a* an explanation of an allusion to the Avesta and its Commentary ('Avasta u Zand'); incidental marginal references to Amīr Khusrau; also a few others, not worthy of particular notice. On the back of the last page, as mentioned above, there is a Persian memorandum in regard to the number of folios and one also as to the purchase of the book.

There are seal impressions on several of the folios. An oval one on fol. 313*b* bears the motto, 'O God, blessings be upon Muḥammad!'; this is likewise twice stamped on fol. 318*b*. On fol. 318*b*, besides this motto-seal, there is an oval signet bearing the name of Muḥammad Ṣādiq, and a small square motto-seal, twice impressed, 'O Muḥammad, help me to understand.' On fol. 389*a* is a double impression of a small square signet bearing the name Ghulām 'Alī.

Subject and Arrangement. — The manuscript, as already stated, contains the collected works of Sa'dī arranged as follows: I. Preface, by 'Alī bin Aḥmad, fol. 2*b*–4*b*. — II. Six *Risālahs*, or Treatises, thus arranged: (*a*) First Risālah, fol. 4*b*–9*a*; (*b*) Second Risālah (though not numbered so in this copy) containing the five *majlises*, or homilies, fol. 9*a*–28*a*; (*c*) Third Risālah (here numbered as second), fol. 28*a*–29*b*; (*d*) Fourth (third) Risālah, fol. 29*b*–32*a*; (*e*) Fifth (fourth) Risālah, fol. 32*a*–42*b*; (*f*) Sixth Risālah, consisting of three short tracts, fol. 42*b*–47*a*.[1] — III. *Gulistān*, fol. 47*b*–130*a*. —

[1] The order of these Risālahs and the beginnings of the subdivisions is the same as that given by Muqtadir and Ross, *Catalogue of Arabic and*

IV. *Būstān,* fol. 130*b*–230*a*. — V. Arabic *Qaṣīdahs,* fol. 230*b*–239*a*. — VI. Persian *Qaṣīdahs,* fol. 239*b*–264*b*. — VII. *Mārs̱'iyāt,* or Elegies, fol. 264*b*–269*b*. — VIII. *Tarjī'āt,* or Refrain Poems, 269*b*–275*a*. — IX. *Ṭayyibāt,* or Pleasant Odes, 275*b*–362*a*. — X. *Badā'i',* or Artificial Odes, 362*b*–403*a*. — XI. *Khawātīm,* or Signet-rings, 403*b*–419*a*. — XII. *Ghazaliyyāt-i Qadīmah,* or Early Odes, fol. 419*b*–427*a*. — XIII. *Ṣāḥibiyyah,* or Epigrammatic Poems in *Muqaṭṭa'āt* form, dedicated to Shams ad-Dīn, Ṣāḥib-Dīwān, fol. 427*b*–450*a*. — XIV. *Muṭayyibāt,* or Jocular Poems, fol. 450*b*–459*a*. — XV. *Muḍḥikāt,* or Facetiae, fol. 459*b*–467*a*. — XVI. *Rubā'iyāt,* or Quatrains, fol. 467*a*–476*b*. — XVII. *Fardiyāt,* or Detached Distichs, fol. 476*b*–479*a*.

Illuminations and Illustrations. — The codex, as stated above, is particularly rich in illuminated 'unwāns, or title-pieces to the numerous works it contains. In addition to these, each page has gilt section-headings adorned with flower patterns and inscribed in white ink, with corner angles that correspond in design. There are twelve illustrative miniatures, usually half-page in size, but two of these which precede the frontispiece and two which follow the last folio are whole-page paintings. All the pictures except that on the first folio are the work of a single artist, whose name, however, is not given. In style these miniatures recall the general characteristics of the Transoxianian school of art; and in certain details, especially the projecting turbans of the women, they remind one of the paintings by an artist named Maḥmūd in a manuscript copied at Bukhārā towards the middle of the sixteenth century, as reproduced by Blochet, *Peintures des manuscrits persans,* pl. 19; compare likewise two of the sixteenth-century miniatures

Persian Manuscripts in the Library at Bankipore, I. 133–136, 145, although the numbering is slightly different.

from Firdausī's *Shāh-nāmah* (polo-match) and Sa'dī's *Gulistān* (Anūshīrwān) in D'Allemagne, *Du Khorassan, compte rendu*, Paris, 1911. <Now compare also four miniatures from a manuscript, dated 1539, reproduced by Martin, *Miniature Painting*, 2. pl. 141–142, and 1. 116–117, by an artist called Shaikh-zādah Maḥmūd.> This would be in accord with the probable date of the introductory full-page painting (fol. 1*b*) by a different artist, also anonymous, as the style of that painting recalls an earlier type of the work represented by 'Alī Naqī, whose three miniatures in the Shāh-nāmah Ms. No. 4 (fol. 24*b*, 100*a*, 102*a*) have been alluded to above. A list of the miniatures and illuminations follows: —

1 fol. 1*b*. The youthful Sa'dī and his teacher Abu'l Faraj ibn al-Jauzī. This is in accordance with the Persian note in minuscule hand at the bottom of the painting, which reads 'The Sage and Sa'dī of Shīrāz.' (The ornamental borders on this and the next page are worthy of special notice.)

2 fol. 2*a*. A ruler in his palace. The ruler represented is probably Sa'dī's patron, Sa'd bin Zangī, the Atābek of Fārs, from whom Sa'dī took his poetical name, and who died in 1226 A.D. (In the illuminated head-piece above the picture are given the titles of three of the *Risālahs*, or prose treatises, that follow. The ornamental borders match those on the preceding page.)

I (*a*) fol. 2*b*. Illuminated full-page title, with an ornate border containing the names of most of the works in the codex.

II (*b*) fol. 4*b*. Inscribed ornamental band and corner angle as titles to the collection of *Risālahs*.

III (*c*) fol. 47*b*. Illuminated title-piece to the *Gulistān*.

3 fol. 89*a*. The head of a village thanks the king for accepting his humble hospitality over night. (To illustrate a story in Sa'dī's *Gulistān*, 3. 20.)

4 fol. 99*b*. A youth in an ordinary station of life, who had lost his heart to a princess, dies at her feet when she speaks to him as she is out riding. (To illustrate a story of youth and love in the *Gulistān*, 5. 4.)

IV (*d*) fol. 130*b*. Illuminated title-piece to the *Būstān*.

5 fol. 152*b*. The servants of one of the monarchs of Ghūr make obeisance before him in joy when they find him after he had been lost all night. (To illustrate a story in Sa'dī's *Būstān*, 1. 678–753.)

6 fol. 204*b*. A man complained to Dā'ūd of Ṭāi that a Ṣūfī mystic was drunk and had fallen in the street; as a rebuke to the informer, for not concealing the faults of another, Dā'ūd bade him bring the man to him on his own back. (To illustrate *Būstān*, 7. 117–133.)

V (*e*) fol. 230*b*. Illuminated title-piece to the Arabic *Qaṣīdahs*.

VI (*f*) fol. 239*b*. Illuminated title-piece to the Persian *Qaṣīdahs*.

7 fol. 252*a*. A lover falls before the feet of his beloved in a wood and praises her. (To illustrate a passage in the Persian *Qaṣīdahs*.)

VII [(*g*) fol. 264*b*. The title-band to the *Elegies* is outlined on the margin, but left blank.]

VIII (*h*) fol. 269*b*. Illuminated title-piece to the *Refrain Poems*.

IX (*i*) fol. 275*b*. Illuminated title-piece to the *Ṭayyibāt*, or Pleasant Odes.

8 fol. 343*a*. A scene of dancing and music. (An illustration for the *Odes*.)

X (*j*) fol. 362*b*. Illuminated title-piece to the *Artificial Odes*.

9 fol. 389*a*. A scene of lovers and their friends in a garden. (To illustrate one of the *Artificial Odes*.)

XI (*k*) fol. 403*b*. Illuminated title-piece to the poems called '*Signet-rings*.'

10 fol. 416*b*. A garden scene. (To illustrate one of the 'Signet-ring' poems.)

XII (*l*) fol. 419*b*. Illuminated title-piece to the *Early Ghazals*.

XIII (*m*) fol. 427*b*. Illuminated title-piece to the *Ṣāḥibiyyah Poems*.

XIV (*n*) fol. 450*b*. Illuminated title-piece to the *Jocular Poems*.

XV (*o*) fol. 459*b*. Illuminated title-piece to the *Muḍḥikāt.*
XVI (*p*) fol. 467*a*. Illuminated title-band to the *Rubā'iyāt.*
XVII (*q*) fol. 476*b*. Small ornamented marginal band to the *Fardiyāt.*
11 fol. 479*b*. Preparing a noonday meal on an outing. (This miniature is directly connected in subject with the one on the next page.)
12 fol. 480*a*. A part of the preceding out-of-door scene; two of the persons are playing chess while the others are differently engaged.

14

Sa'dī: Būstān, or 'Garden of Perfume.' An illustrated and illuminated manuscript, of not later date than the second quarter of the seventeenth century, very beautifully written and embellished by highly ornate borders. The copy is particularly interesting because, as is known from the seals and memorandums, it was a much-read volume in the royal library of the Mughal Emperor Shāh Jahān and of his son Aurangzīb.

Size. — $9\frac{3}{4} \times 6\frac{1}{2}$ in. (24.7×16.5 cm.); written surface, $6\frac{1}{2} \times 3\frac{1}{2}$ in. (16.5×8.7 cm.); the covers are not the original ones and they measure considerably larger than the pages. Folios 158, the last page being blank. There are no folios missing; in two instances, however (fol. 13*b* and 57*b*), the catchword is wrongly taken from the beginning of the second line on the following page instead of from the first line, but nothing is wanting. Five folios are misbound between folios 43 and 49; the proper order should be fol. 45, 44, 48, 46, 47, instead of the present arrangement.

Binding. — Recased in ordinary Oriental flap-covers of red leather. The original binding must have been different, for it is spoken of in a Persian memorandum (see *F* below) on the last page, made by one of the royal librarians and dated in 1649 A.D., as 'a cover of smooth (*raughanī*, lit. 'oleose, oily, or glossy') leather.'

Writing and Paper. — The handwriting is an extremely handsome Nasta'līq, and is particularly mentioned in the royal librarian's memorandum (*F*), as noted below. The copy is written 14 lines to a page in two gold-ruled columns. The paper is of a heavy quality, and the written part of each folio is inset with perfect skill in a highly ornate broad border described below.

Date and Scribe. — The manuscript is not dated in the colophon, but, judging from the seals and memorandums, the earliest one (see *A* below) being dated in 1647 A.D., it probably belongs to the earlier half of Shāh Jahān's reign, or the second quarter of the seventeenth century. The name of the scribe is given in the colophon as Pāyandah Muḥammad.

Memorandums. — The front and back folios are covered with seals and memorandums in Persian which show that the manuscript belonged to the library of the Mughal Emperor Shāh Jahān and of his sŏn Aurangzīb. Two of these seals on the first page and three on the last bear Shāh Jahān's name, joined each time with that of a different court official; and Aurangzīb's signet on the first page and on the last is each time combined also with a different official's name. The seals appear to have been stamped at various times (the intervals sometimes being short), and the memorandums added, by custodians of the Imperial Library, as noted below. The probable order in which the signets were impressed, so far as can be judged from their position and certain dates in memorandums nearby, is as follows: —

Seal 1. (First page, lower large seal.) This seal reads: 'Shāh Jahān — Ṣāliḥ was his Murshid [*i.e.* preceptor and spiritual guide].'[1] This Ṣāliḥ was one of the preceptors at court, as his name is mentioned by the Venetian physician Manucci as the tutor of Shāh Jahān's son, Aurangzīb. He had received a pension from Shāh Jahān and had expected a larger stipend when his former pupil, Aurangzīb, came to the throne. He was rebuffed, however, and was sent off in disgrace because Aurangzīb remembered his teaching only with dissatisfaction (see Manucci, *Storia do Mogor, or Mogul India*, translated by G. W. Irvine, 2. 29–33, London, 1906; possibly compare also Sachau and Ethé, *Cat. Pers. Mss. Bodl. Lib.*, col. 683, no. 1094).

Seal 2. (Last page, lower left seal.) This reads: 'Shāh Jahān, Pādishāh of Divine Sovereignty. The devoted Murīd, Sayyid (?) Aḥmad.' The title *murīd* for a divinity student is explained in the footnote below.

Seal 3. (Last page, upper left seal.) This is the same as seal 1 and reads: 'Shāh Jahān — Ṣāliḥ was his Murshid.'

Seal 4. (Last page, upper right seal.) 'Shāh Jahān's Murshid [*i.e.* preceptor] was Muḥammad 'Alī.'

Seal 5. (First page, upper right seal.) This seal reads 'Shāh Jahān — 'Ināiat Khān, 1068 A.H. [= 1658 A.D.].' This 'Ināiat Khān was doubtless the same one who, as is known from the contemporary court records, was employed in the office of the Imperial Library of Shāh Jahān. He was the author of a history of Shāh Jahān's reign, the *Shāh-Jahān-nāmah*, as well as of other works; and a notice of him says: 'He was witty and of agreeable manners, and was one of the intimate friends of Shāh Jahān; latterly he retired from office and settled in Kashmīr, where he died, 1077 A.H. [= 1666 A.D.].' (See Elliot, *History of India*, 7. 73–74; compare likewise Beale, *Oriental Biographical Dictionary*, p. 179, London,

[1] The word *murshid*, 'leader, instructor, spiritual guide, monitor,' is a title given to a member of a higher religious order, especially of the Ṣūfīs. The word *murīd*, lit. 'one who is desirous,' denotes a pupil or disciple of such a spiritual guide, a divinity student, or aspirant for higher religious knowledge in the advanced order to which his superior belongs.

1894; also Sachau and Ethé, *Cat. Pers. Mss. Bodl. Lib.*, col. 457, no. 513.)

Seal 6. (Last page, middle left seal.) Illegible, but beside it is a memorandum (*I*, as given below), dated Dhī'l-Hajjah 18, 1068 A.H. = Sept. 16, 1658 A.D., or three months after Shāh Jahān had been shut up in his palace as a prisoner by his son Aurangzīb.

Seal 7. (Last page, middle right seal.) The darkly inked signet, containing the name of Aurangzīb, who was called also 'Ālam-gīr, 'World-controller,' reads: ''Ālam Gīr, Pādishāh. . . . [*illegible*] Khān.'

Seal 8. (First page, upper left seal.) This likewise contains Aurangzīb's name and a co-signature, and reads: ''Ālam Gīr, Pādishāh. — Sayyid 'Alī al-Ḥusainī, Murīd [*i.e.* the divinity student].'

Seal 9. (First page, lower left.) This smaller dark seal is illegible as regards the name, but contains the title 'the Servant of the Court,' showing that it was stamped by a royal official.

Seal 10. (First page, center seal.) This pear-shaped seal of apparently later date is so badly stamped that too few letters are legible to allow it to be deciphered.

Seal 11. (Last folio, 158*a*, near colophon.) A small oval seal bearing the name of Shukr Khān — twice repeated. Two other seals near it have been obliterated.

Seal 12. (Front fly-leaf, upper left seal.) This small octagonal seal is dated in the last quarter of the eighteenth century and contains a verse from the Qur'ān (14. 7), 'If ye be thankful I shall give you increase — 1203 A.H. [= 1788–1789 A.D.].'

There are a large number of special memorandums, mostly adjacent to the seals; they were doubtless added by the custodians of the Imperial Library in connection with the intrusting or transferring (*taḥwīl*) of the manuscript from the keeping of one official to that of another, either at the time of a change of office or for some special consignment. Further notes as to the inspection of the book at such times or its perusal on particular occasions (*'arḍ-dīdah*) are still more frequently added, sometimes in connection with the seal, but sometimes without any signature or seal, although the date is always recorded.[1] In several instances the handwriting in these memorandums is by one and the same individual. The order of these notations, judging from the dates, is approximately as follows: —

A. (Memorandum, first page, bottom, below seal 1 of Shāh Jahān.) This memorandum reads: 'Būstān was intrusted (*taḥwīl*) to Khwājah Shihāb, for the use of the divinity students (*murīdān*), first day of Dhī'l-Hajjah, year 20th of the Blessed Reign, corresponding to the year 1056 Hijri [*i.e.* Jan. 8, 1647 A.D.]. — Value one hundred pieces [*i.e.* rupees].' This Khwājah Shihāb is the same person to whom the book was again intrusted three years later (year 23d of the reign), as is recorded in a memorandum near the top of the last page, and he is probably the Shihāb whose name appears on a seal dated with 'the year 23,' mentioned in the catalogue of Pertsch, *Handschriften der königlichen Bibliothek zu Berlin, Pers. Hss.*, p. 857–858, Berlin, 1888. One might possibly suggest that this Shihāb was the same as Shihāb ad-Dīn Aḥmad Tālish, who wrote a history of Aurangzīb in 1662 A.D., cf. Beale, *Oriental Biographical Dictionary*, p. 360.

B. (Memorandum, last page, to right of seal 2 of Shāh Jahān.) This memorandum reads: 'Intrusted (*taḥwīl*) to Muḥammad Manṣūr, 25th of the month Ṣafar, year 21 [*i.e.* 1057 A.H. = April 1, 1647 A.D.]. Value one hundred pieces and fifty [*i.e.* 150 rupees].'

C. (Memorandum, first page, to left of illegible seal 10.) 'Inspected [or perused] (*'arḍ-dīdah shud*) 22 of Jumāda aṣ-Ṣānī, year 21 [*i.e.* 1057 A.H. = July 25, 1647 A.D.].'

D. (Memorandum, last page, bottom, under seal 2 of Shāh Jahān.) 'Inspected [or perused] (*'arḍ-dīdah shud*) . . . of Rabī' al-Awwal, year 22 [*i.e.* 1058 A.H. = March–April, 1648 A.D.].'

[1] Such appears to be the usage of the terms *taḥwīl* and *'arḍ-dīdah*. Professor Edward G. Browne, of Cambridge, England, in a letter kindly communicated on the subject, rightly observes that these terms are peculiar to India and to manuscripts of Indian origin.

E. (Memorandum, last page, left top, over seal 3 of Shāh Jahān.) 'Inspected [or perused], the second of the blessed (month) of Ramaḍān, in the year 22 [*i.e.* 1058 A.H. = Sept. 20, 1648 A.D.].'

F. (Last page, top right, near seal 4 of Shāh Jahān.) This is a palimpsest inscription, the former writing having been practically erased. The memorandum as preserved contains a double item, the first being a brief description of the book; to this is added a second note as to its being consigned or intrusted. The whole reads as follows: 'Būstān, in elegant script, white paper, margins inlaid, cover of smooth leather . . . [*illegible*]. — It was intrusted (*taḥwīl*) to Khwājah Shihāb for the divinity students (*murīdān*) on the . . . of Dhī'l-Hajjah, the year 23 of the Blessed Reign [*i.e.* 1059 A.H. = Dec. —, 1649 A.D.]. Value one hundred rupees.' On Shihāb see above, memorandum *A*.

G. (Memorandum in center of last page.) 'Inspected [or perused], 24th of the month Sha'bān, the year 25 of the Blessed Reign [*i.e.* 1061 A.H. = Aug. 12, 1651].'

H. (Memorandum, last page, lower right-hand corner.) 'Inspected [or perused], 23d of Dhī-Hajjah, year 26 [*i.e.* 1062 A.H. = Nov. 25, 1652].'

I. (Memorandum, first page, lower right.) 'Inspected [or perused], 17 (? or 7) of Rabī' al-Awwal, year 30 [*i.e.* 1066 A.H. = Jan. 14 (? or 4), 1656 A.D.].'

J. (Memorandum, first page, upper right, below seal 5 of Shāh Jahān.) 'Inspected [or perused], 23d of Jumāda aṣ-Ṣānī, year 32 [*i.e.* 1068 A.H. = March 28, 1658].'

K. (Memorandum, last page, right hand margin, below seal 7 of 'Ālam-gīr.) 'Was intrusted (*taḥwīl*) to Mun'im Beg, 9th of Rajab, year 32 [*i.e.* 1068 A.H. = April 12, 1658].' (It might be hazardous to try to connect this Mun'im Beg with the poet-soldier Mun'im Shaikh, who is recorded as fighting in a battle the next year, Dec. 1659; cf. Beale, *Or. Biog. Dict.*, p. 279.)

L. (Memorandum, last page, middle left, near illegible seal 6.) 'Inspected [or perused] (*'arḍ-dīdah shud*) 18th of Dhī'l-Hajjah, year 1068 = 32 (reign) [*i.e.* Sept. 16, 1658].'

M. (Memorandum, first page, lower left margin, near seal 9.) 'Inspected [or perused], 17th of Rabī' aṣ-Ṣānī, year 1069 A.H. [= Jan. 12, 1659].'

X. (Small memorandum, last page, lower right, just above memorandum *H.*) 'Inspected [or perused], 16th of Ṣafar, year 7 (?) [*i.e.* probably of Aurangzīb's reign, or about Sept. 8, 1664 A.D.].'

Y. (Memorandum, last page, middle right, or slightly below and to the left of Aurangzīb's seal 7.) 'Inspected [or perused], 12th of Rajab, year 13 [probably of Aurangzīb's reign, *i.e.* 1082 A.H. = Nov. 14, 1671].'

Z. (Memorandum, last page, below seal 2.) The dates are obliterated so that the year can not be determined. The memorandum, so far as it can be deciphered, reads: 'It was intrusted (*taḥwīl*) to . . . Value, one hundred rupees.'

Fly-leaf. On the fly-leaf, in addition to the seal (12) described above, there are three incidental jottings by later hands. That to the right has six verses from a Persian mystic love poem. The one to the lower left is another Persian memorandum stating: 'The book of Būstān was purchased from Karīm Khān Qanbaralī through the kindness of . . . for . . . [*price obliterated*].' The third note, just below the small seal, contains a prayer in behalf of some one who has died; it reads: 'Then the Hand of Providence carried the poor servant . . . [*name erased*] to his destination; may God establish his honor!'

Other memorandums. There are a few memorandums of no importance written by a later hand in black ink at the top of four or five pages, for example, the title of the chapter in only two cases, fol. 67*a*, 81*b*, and the title of the poetic story in merely two or three instances.

Subject. — The celebrated poetic work of Sa'dī, written in 1257 A.D., in ten chapters, as follows: — (*a*) Introduction, fol. 1*b*–8*b*. — I. First Chapter, On Justice and Government, fol. 8*b*–48*b*. — II. Second Chapter, On Benevolence, fol. 48*a*–66*b*. — III. Third Chapter, On Love, fol. 67*a*–81*a*. — IV. Fourth Chapter, On Humility, fol. 81*a*–102*b*. — V. Fifth Chapter, On Resignation, fol. 102*b*–110*b*. — VI. Sixth Chapter, On Contentment, fol. 110*b*–115*b*. — VII. Seventh Chapter, On Education, fol. 115*b*–133*a*. — VIII. Eighth Chapter, On Gratitude, fol. 133*a*–143*a*. —

IX. Ninth Ċhapter, On Repentance, fol. 143*a*–154*a*. — X. Tenth Chapter, On Prayer, fol. 154*a*–158*a*.

Illuminations and Illustrations. — The copy is noteworthy for the elaborate decoration of its inlaid borders. The broad margins are ornamented with gold flowered designs of the greatest variety, no two pages being exactly alike, though similar in effect. Colored vignettes of different patterns and varying shades of yellow, blue, and green are then inset, five vignettes to a page, and adorned with gilded traceries. The section-headings, one or more on each folio, are written in red ink and heightened by gold filigree work. There is also a small 'unwān at the beginning of the book.

The three miniatures which illustrate the manuscript are the work of a single artist, but no name is given. In the point of the expression of the faces they are better than in the matter of execution or design; in certain traits they recall features of the Transoxianian style, but in many respects they are unique. Especially noteworthy is the delineation of the nose, particularly on fol. 47*a*. The subjects illustrated are as follows: —

I (*a*) fol. 1*b*. Small illuminated title-piece to the *Būstān*.

1 fol. 30*b*. A religious devotee, who was summoned to pray for the king's recovery, says that his prayer will do no good unless the king releases all prisoners and provides alms for the poor.

2 fol. 47*a*. A Fire-worshiper was received at the board of Abraham the Patriarch, but as the Gabr began to eat without first giving thanks to God, Abraham ejected him from the house. (The figure of Abraham is recognizable by the nimbus around the head.)

3 fol. 94*b*. King Ṣāliḥ of Syria entertaining two dervishes in his palace. (For King Ṣāliḥ see d'Herbelot, *Bibliothèque orientale*, 3. 173, The Hague, 1778.)

V

THE INDO-PERSIAN POET

AMĪR KHUSRAU OF DELHĪ

BAHRAM GUR IN THE RED PALACE
Ms. No. 15, fol. 159*a* (see page 123)

AMĪR KHUSRAU OF DELHĪ

(1253–1325 A.D.)

Amīr Khusrau of Delhī, India's greatest Persian poet, was an imitator of Niẓāmī, the romantic poet of Persia, and lived at the court of the Khaljī Monarch, 'Alā ad-Dīn, of Delhī, India, where he died, Nov. 6, 1325, and where his tomb is still shown in the environs of the older city.

Amīr Khusrau's *Khamsah*, or 'Quintet,' is modeled on the work of his famous Persian romantic predecessor, though with an individuality still his own. The titles and dates of these five works are as follows: 1. *Maṭla' al-Anwār*, or 'Rising of the Luminaries,' corresponding to Niẓāmī's *Makhzan al-Asrār*, and written by Amīr Khusrau in 698 A.H. = 1298 A.D. — 2. *Shīrīn u Khusrau*, an imitation of Niẓāmī's romantic epopee on the love of King Khusrau of Persia and the fair Shīrīn, written by Amīr Khusrau, 698 A.H. = 1298 A.D. — 3. *Majnūn u Lailā*, also an imitation of Niẓāmī's poem of the same name, and finished in 698 A.H. = 1298–1299 A.D. — 4. *Ā'īnah-i Iskandarī*, or 'Mirror of Alexander the Great,' parallel with Niẓāmī's *Iskandar-nāmah*, and finished in 699 A.H. = 1299 A.D. — 5. *Hasht Bahisht*, or 'Eight Paradises,' the eight love-romances of the Sāsānian King Bahrām Gūr, written in 701 A.H. = 1302 A.D. All of these works, with the exception of the *Hasht Bahisht*, were dedicated to the Khaljī ruler of India, Sulṭān 'Alā ad-Dīn (1296–1316 A.D.). Amīr Khusrau was the author likewise of several other poems, notably a collection of lyrics that antedate Ḥāfiẓ in point of time, and of poems on historic and romantic events connected with his own contemporaries in high positions.

In the present manuscript the order of the last two of the five romances is inverted and follows Niẓāmī's arrangement rather than the chronological order of Amīr Khusrau's work.[1]

[1] In this particular copy, moreover, the date of composition is included in only three of the poems, namely in *Shīrīn and Khusrau*, on fol. 102*b*,

15

Amīr Khusrau of Delhī: Khamsah, or 'Quintet,' five romantic poems modeled upon Niẓāmī. A very beautiful small manuscript in Indian-Persian style, not dated, but belonging to the latter half of the seventeenth century, the period of the later Mughal court. The seventeen exquisite miniatures which adorn the work are, for the most part, signed, and the majority of them are by a single artist, Muḥammad Salīm, who appears to have been a painter at the court of the Mughal Emperor Aurangzīb; three others bear the signatures of two different artists.

Size. — $7\frac{3}{4} \times 5$ in. (19.6 × 12.5 cm.); written surface, $6\frac{3}{8} \times 3\frac{5}{8}$ in. (16.2 × 9.2 cm.). Folios 246, including a blank page or even two and more after each of the five poems. Three folios are missing, one each after fol. 149, 151, 211.

Binding. — Rebound in old red morocco, bordered with a flowered band of gilt; the inside covers are of a simple dark green leather, requiring no special comment.

Writing and Paper. — Written in a handsome small Nasta'līq script, 19 lines to a page in four columns, gold-ruled and containing frequent rubric captions together with pink interlineations in the verses above and below the miniatures. The paper is of an exceptionally fine Indian quality and has the effect of vellum; a heavier weight paper is used for the pages containing the miniatures, except in the case

as 698 A.H. = 1298 A.D.; in *Majnūn and Lailā*, on fol. 138*a*, as the same year (698 A.H.) although there is a mistake in the copying of the wording, 'six hundred and ninety sixty,' the last Persian word *shast*, 'sixty,' having been erroneously copied instead of *hasht*, 'eight'; finally, in *Ā'īnah-i Iskandarī*, on fol. 245*a*, in words as 'one less than nine (!) hundred,' an error for one less than seven hundred, *i.e.* 699 A.H. = 1299 A.D.

of the first picture. The written surface of all the pages is lightly sprinkled with gold.

Date and Scribe. — Not mentioned in the body of the text, although it may be reasonably gathered from external and internal evidence that the manuscript was written in the latter half of the seventeenth century and by Mullā Muḥammad Amīn, as explained in the footnote below.[1]

Memorandums. — As observed in the footnote below, there is on the back of the first illuminated page a Persian memorandum, '*Khamsah* (Quintet) of Khwājah Khusrau in the handwriting of Mullā Amīn,' and similarly on the label on the back of the binding. The title of each poem is

[1] The evidence, which seems plausible, is as follows: Seven out of a dozen miniatures, which are practically identical in style, are signed by the artist Muḥammad Salīm, as already noted and as will be further explained below; one (134*b*) is signed as 'by a substitute for Muḥammad,' the artist giving only Muḥammad's name and remaining himself anonymous. The style of all of the paintings by Muḥammad Salīm recalls directly that of the miniatures made by an artist Muḥammad for the Venetian Nicolao Manucci, who was court physician to Aurangzīb (reigned in 1659–1680), and who left India in 1690, carrying with him a collection of portraits from this painter's brush. Of him Manucci says: 'The artist was a friend of mine, Mīr [*i.e.* the noble] Muḥammad, an official in the household of prince Shāh 'Ālam' (see Manucci, *Storia do Mogor, or Mogul India*, translated by G. W. Irvine, 1. p. liv, London, 1906; and compare Blochet, *Peintures de manuscrits arabes, persans, et turcs*, p. 26, Paris, 1911). It seems plausible to conjecture, especially from the style, that the artist is the same as the one referred to by Manucci, and the time would thus be in the reign of Aurangzīb. The scribe's name appears to have been Mullā Muḥammad Amīn, if the name be correctly given in the Persian memorandum on the back of the first illumination, fol. 1*a*, as 'by the handwriting of Mullā Amīn' and then repeated on the label on the back of the binding as 'by the handwriting of Muḥammad Amīn.' There may be some possibility that this was the same as the Mullā Muḥammad Amīn to whom is ascribed the compilation of the Dabistān, shortly before Aurangzīb came to the throne (cf. Rieu, *Cat. Pers. Mss.*, 1. 142). If so, it would accord with the date assigned; but the point is not strongly urged.

jotted in Persian on the blank page before it begins. On the last folio (246*a*) is a small oval seal of an owner whose name was Shāh Rukh.

Subject and Arrangement. — The 'Quintet' already described, arranged as follows: I. *Maṭla' al-Anwār* (fol. 1*b*–44*a*). — II. *Shīrīn u Khusrau* (fol. 46*b*–102*b*). — III. *Majnūn u Lailā* (fol. 103*b*–138*b*). — IV. *Hasht Bahisht* (fol. 139*b*–185*a*). — V. *Ā'īnah-i Iskandarī* (fol. 186*b*–246*a*).

Illuminations and Illustrations. — There are two beautiful 'unwāns as frontispieces to the manuscript and also smaller ones, equally fine, as title-pieces to the five books. The frequent rubric letterings and pink interlineations have been already referred to. The miniatures, seventeen in number, are particularly fine, especially the portraits, which are characteristic of the period of Mughal art. Seven of these paintings (fol. 4*b*, 54*a*, 68*a*, 94*a*, 128*a*, 177*b*, 200*a*) are signed by the artist Muḥammad Salīm; a conjecture has been made in the footnote above as to the possibility of identifying him with the artist at Aurangzīb's court who did the miniatures for Manucci; it is likewise probable that this Muḥammad painted also the miniatures on fol. 81*a*, 111*a*, 120*a*, 156*a*, and 159*a*, though the signature is missing. The miniature on 134*b* is marked as the work of 'a substitute for Muḥammad,' but the artist's own name is not given; he may possibly have painted 172*a*, though that has been retouched. Two other miniatures, 165*a* and 206*b*, are signed by another artist whose name was Lāchīn. The subjects of the miniatures are as follows:

I (*a*–*b*)	fol. 1*b*–2*a*.	Illuminated title-pages to *Maṭla' al-Anwār*.
1	fol. 4*b*.	Muḥammad's ascent to heaven in a vision. Signed in the crown by Muḥammad Salīm.
II (*c*)	fol. 46*b*.	Title-heading to *Shīrīn and Khusrau*.
2	fol. 54*a*.	Khusrau beholds a portrait of Shīrīn, which

had been drawn by a Chinese artist. Signed near the bottom by Muḥammad Salīm.

3 fol. 68*a*. Shīrīn goes on horseback to see the marvelous carvings on the rocks by her sculptor-admirer, Farhād. Signed above the rock by Muḥammad Salīm.

4 fol. 81*a*. Khusrau's skill in hunting.

5 fol. 94*a*. Khusrau and Shīrīn in the palace. Signed at the bottom by Muḥammad Salīm.

III (*d*) fol. 103*b*. Title-heading to *Majnūn and Lailā*.

6 fol. 111*a*. Lailā and Majnūn in love as school-children.

7 fol. 120*a*. Majnūn, the distraught lover, as a recluse.

8 fol. 128*a*. Lailā visits Majnūn in the wilderness. Signed near the bottom by Muḥammad Salīm.

9 fol. 134*b*. Death of Lailā. Signed at the bottom by a 'substitute for Muḥammad.'

IV (*e*) fol. 139*b*. Title-heading of *Hasht Bahisht*.

10 fol. 156*a*. Bahrām Gūr in the Green Palace.

11 fol. 159*a*. Bahrām Gūr in the Red Palace.

12 fol. 165*a*. Bahrām Gūr in the Purple Palace. Signed on the vase by Lāchīn.

13 fol. 172*a*. Bahrām Gūr in the Sandal Palace.

14 fol. 177*b*. Bahrām Gūr in the Camphor-colored Palace. Signed on the steps by Muḥammad Salīm.

V (*f*) fol. 186*b*. Title-page of *Ā'īnah-i Iskandarī*.

15 fol. 200*a*. Alexander in battle with the Kipchaks of China. Signed at the bottom by Muḥammad Salīm.

16 fol. 206*b*. Alexander breaks the arm of the Ruler of the Kipchaks of China. Signed near the lower right-hand corner by Lāchīn.

17 fol. 233*b*. Alexander and his ship on the 'Western Sea near Damascus.'

VI

ḤĀFIẒ

ḤĀFIẒ

(*c.* 1325–*c.* 1389 A.D.)

Ḥāfiẓ, Persia's famous lyric poet and one of the great lyrists of the world, was born in Shīrāz, a city in Southern Persia that had given birth to his renowned predecessor Sa'dī. The real name of Ḥāfiẓ was Muḥammad Shams ad-Dīn, but he is known to fame by the title of *Ḥāfiẓ*, an attribute which signifies 'having a retentive memory,' and which was bestowed upon him as a student 'who knew the whole Qur'ān by heart.'

So talented a scholar would naturally win, as did Ḥāfiẓ, the cultured patronage of the princes and rulers of the line that held sway in Shīrāz and over Southern Persia. A number of them are mentioned in his odes; among them (see below) were Shāh Shujā' and Shāh Manṣūr, but especially the former ruler's able vizir, Khwājah Qiwām ad-Dīn (d. 1363), who was the poet's particular friend and benefactor. This last-named patron founded a Muḥammadan theological academy in honor of Ḥāfiẓ, and in this institution the poet held a professorial chair for a time. His severance from that position appears to have been owing, on the one hand, to his anacreontic, or amatory and convivial, tendencies, and on the other, to his outspoken denunciation of the hypocrisy which characterized some of the Muslim priests in his day.

But gifts like those of Ḥāfiẓ stood in no danger of being overlooked. His poetic fame in due time called forth flattering invitations from dignitaries abroad, one of them being royal solicitation from Maḥmūd Shāh II, of the Bahmanid dynasty in India, to make a sojourn at his court. So high a compliment could not be declined, and Ḥāfiẓ set out for Hindustān. A part of the journey, however, involved a voyage by sea, and at the outset occurred so violent a storm that the poet turned back, abandoned his planned visit, and returned to his home in Shīrāz, which he never afterwards left. It should be added, however, that in graceful recognition of the favor of his would-be patron, he wrote an ode apologizing for not having finally been able to accept the distinguished call.

Ḥāfiẓ was married and there is a mention of sons in his verse. He appears to have lived to a ripe old age, and his death occurred about the year 1389 A.D., although that date is not wholly certain. His tomb lies in a beautiful garden in the environs of his beloved city of Shīrāz, with whose charms his odes are so closely linked.

Love and wine, and the nightingale and the rose, form the burden of his lyric songs; but there is considerable difference of opinion, especially in the Occident, regarding the manner in which these tender, passionate effusions are to be interpreted. Ḥāfiẓ is often called 'the Persian Anacreon,' and there can be no doubt that there is much that is anacreontic in his verses; at the same time considerable weight must justly be given to the common Oriental interpretation of them, by the mystic Ṣūfīs, as symbolic or allegorical expressions of Divine Love under the guise of human passion. The view, therefore, that is probably nearest the truth is that which holds the mean between the extremes in interpreting the odes of this profoundly human and ideally poetic master of lyric song.

Translations of Ḥāfiẓ have been made into many languages and he has influenced the poets of many lands (compare the bibliography in Ethé, *Neupersische Litteratur*, p. 303–305). Most valuable and complete in its scope is the English version, with commentary, by H. Wilberforce Clarke, *The Dīwān-i Ḥāfiẓ*, London, 1891; consult also Bicknell, *Hafiz*, London, 1875; Robinson, *Persian Poetry for English Readers*, p. 384–507, London, 1883; McCarthy, *Ghazals of Hafiz*, New York, 1893; Bell, *Poems from the Divan of Hafiz*, London, 1897; Leaf, *Versions from Hafiz*, London, 1898; and especially Payne, *Hafiz*, 1901; see furthermore, Pizzi, *Storia della poesia persiana*, I. 302–347, Turin, 1894; Horn, *Geschichte der persischen Litteratur*, p. 114–122, Leipzig, 1901; F. Veit, *Platens Nachbildungen aus dem Diwan des Hafiz*, Berlin, 1908.

16

Ḥāfiẓ: Dīwān, or complete poetical works of Ḥāfiẓ, the great lyric poet of Persia. An interesting small manuscript belonging approximately to the end of the eighteenth or the beginning of the nineteenth century. It is rich in miniatures, seventy-five in number, painted in one of the typical styles of Persian art. The white-bearded man that figures in almost all the illustrations appears to represent Ḥāfiẓ in his older years.

Size. — $7\frac{1}{4} \times 4\frac{1}{4}$ in. (= 18.0×10.7 cm.); written surface, $5\frac{1}{4} \times 2\frac{7}{8}$ in. (= 13.9×7.4 cm.). Folios 365, numbered in Persian figures. To this count should be added the seven folios of the Preface, which are not numbered, though apparently copied by the same hand.

Binding. — Rebound in a very dark brown Oriental leather, with stitched woven bands in Shīrāzī style, and with tissues bound in opposite the illustrations. The inner covers are overspread with a plain dull crimson leather.

Writing and Paper. — Good, clear Nastaʿlīq, 11 lines to a page, in two columns separated by an ornamental tendril band and framed in rulings of gold, green, red, and blue, with a marginal line of gold and black beyond; a powdering of gold-dust heightens the written surface. The name of Ḥāfiẓ in the various poems is always written in red ink. The paper is of a very fine light quality; the fly-leaves are of a slightly heavier texture.

Date and Scribe. — No date or name of copyist is given, as there is no colophon, but the manuscript appears to belong to the late eighteenth or early nineteenth century (more probably the latter), and it may have been copied at Shīrāz, if an inference may be drawn from the general style.

Memorandums. — On the three introductory fly-leaves are verses in Persian, by a later hand, on Tamerlane (1333–1405), on Fātiḥ, and on Ḥāfiẓ's patron, Shāh Shujā' of Shīrāz (d. 1384). On the first page (and obliterated on next to the last fly-leaf) is stamped in carmine ink the seal of an owner, whose name was Shafī'. On the top of the last page is a Persian memorandum that the manuscript contains 'seventy-five (75) miniature paintings.' This number is correct.

Subject and Arrangement. — The *Dīwān*, or Collected Lyric Poems, of Ḥāfiẓ, introduced by the Preface of Gulandām (cf. Rieu, *Cat. Pers. Mss. Brit. Mus.*, p. 627–628), and arranged as follows: (i) Gulandām's *Preface* to Ḥāfiẓ's works, fol. i*b*–vii*b*. — I. *Ghazals*, or Odes, five hundred and ninety-seven in number, fol. 1*b*–316*b*; among these are poems in praise of several rulers or notables in the time of Ḥāfiẓ, for example of Shāh Manṣūr Muẓaffar (d. 1392), fol. 116*a*–116*b*; of Ḥāfiẓ's own patron Shāh Shujā' (d. 1384), on fol. 186*a*–187*a*; of Yaḥyā ibn Muẓaffar (1353–1430 A.D.), ruler of Shīrāz, fol. 196*a*–197*b*; of Manṣūr ibn Muḥammad of Shīrāz, fol. 210*a*–211*b*; of Khwājah Tūrān Shāh (d. 1385), who was vizir to the patron of Ḥāfiẓ, fol. 233*b*–234*b*; again of Shāh Shujā', fol. 249*b*–251*b*; of Nuṣrat ad-Dīn Yaḥyā, of Shīrāz, fol. 265*a*–266*a*; and of the same, fol. 270*b*–271*b*; of Muḥammad ibn 'Alī, fol. 298*b*–300*a*; again of the above-mentioned Khwājah Tūrān Shāh, fol. 305*a*–305*b*; and lastly of Khwājah Qiwām ad-Dīn, fol. 345*a* and 350*a*. — II. Three *Maṣnawīs*, or Poems in Rimed Couplets, beginning *Alā ai āhū-i*, fol. 316*b*–324*b*. — III. *Mughannī-nāmah*, or Singer's Book, beginning *Biyā Sāqī*, fol. 325*a*–331*b*. — IV. *Tarjī'-band*, or Refrains, beginning *Ai dādah ba-bād*, fol. 331*b*–334*b*. — V. *Qaṣīdahs*, or Panegyrics, beginning *Māhī chū tū*, fol. 334*b*–337*a*. — VI. *Mukhammas*, or Quintuple Rimes, fol. 337*a*–338*b*. — VII. *Muqaṭṭa'āt*, or

Miscellaneous Fragments, fol. 338*b*–351*a*.—VIII. *Rubā'iyāt*, or Quatrains, one hundred and twelve in number, arranged in nearly alphabetical order, fol. 351*a*–365*b*.

Illuminations and Illustrations. — The *Preface* is introduced by a less ornate title-piece; the *Dīwān* itself opens with two highly embellished full-page 'unwāns, gold and green predominating in the decoration. Throughout the work there are flowered bands and countless small floral panels marking the end of each ode, quatrain, or series of verses. The seventy-five miniatures which illustrate the various subjects of the poems are nearly full-page in size, and are the work of a single artist in a strongly marked Persian style. The white-bearded man who appears throughout in the illustrations, as noted above, may be assumed to represent a conception of Ḥāfiẓ in his older years. To be observed also is the frequent occurrence of the slender dark cypress tree and of the rose bush and the nightingale in pictures illustrative of the lyric verses. The main details as to the illuminations and paintings are as follows: —

i (*a*) fol. 1*b*. Simple illuminated title to the *Preface* to Ḥāfiẓ by Gulandām.

I (*b–c*) fol. 1*b*–2*a*. Double illuminated title-page and introduction to the *Ghazals*, or Odes; in these two embellishments, gold and green combine as predominant colors.

1 fol. 4*a*. Ascent of Muḥammad to heaven in a vision.

2 fol. 5*a*. 'Look into the Cup of Jamshīd and the Mirror of Alexander in order to have an insight into the Kingdom of Darius' — so says Ḥāfiẓ to his friend.

3 fol. 6*a*. 'Why turn to Mecca when our venerable sage turns to the wine-house?'

4 fol. 8*b*. God's providence saves after tribulations, as shown in the lives of the Patriarchs of old.

5 fol. 12*b*. If Ḥāfiẓ has his friend he cares not, though he be crucified like Manṣūr.

6 fol. 13*b*. It is the hour of pleasure, the beloved friend joins

in the wine-drinking, and the musicians are playing.

7 fol. 15*b*. Ḥāfiẓ meets his sweetheart, who is on horseback.

8 fol. 17*b*. Sulṭān Maḥmūd and his favorite Ayāz; also Lailā and Majnūn. (All four are mentioned in the Ode.)

9 fol. 20*a*. Ḥāfiẓ's sweetheart departs with her handmaidens.

10 fol. 21*a*. Ḥāfiẓ grieving for his absent sweetheart.

11 fol. 24*b*. Ḥāfiẓ's loss of his beloved is likened to the loss of Solomon's seal.

12 fol. 26*a*. Ḥāfiẓ, a student of love, is no more to be blamed than the Shaikh of Ṣan'ān who pawned his cloak in the wine-shop but still praised God.

13 fol. 27*b*. Ḥāfiẓ likens the shadow of his cypress-like sweetheart to the reflection of the Divine Spirit.

14 fol. 29*b*. The happy night of union with the beloved.

15 fol. 31*b*. Ḥāfiẓ says: 'The time of Majnūn the lover has passed; it is now our turn.'

16 fol. 38*b*. 'Shīrīn is the only subject of Farhād's talk, and Lailā's curl is the abode of Majnūn.' (These four lovers are portrayed in the picture.)

17 fol. 41*a*. The beloved of Ḥāfiẓ kneels by his pillow at night.

18 fol. 45*a*. 'Do not rely on the wind; even though now it blows the way you wish — soaring like Solomon on his throne by the aid of the *dīvs* (demons) — it may later lead to destruction.'

19 fol. 47*a*. Ḥāfiẓ apostrophizing the deserted throne of Jamshīd.

20 fol. 53*a*. Ḥāfiẓ's advice — 'Beware! the beloved, while attentive to thee, may smile behind the veil at another.'

21 fol. 57*b*. Ḥāfiẓ's sweetheart forsakes him.

22 fol. 61*b*. 'Miss not your opportunity for joy: for no one will open the door for you if you lose your key.'

23 fol. 63*b*. Ḥāfiẓ fears that his excessive love may make others jealous of him, as Joseph's beautiful coat aroused the envy of his brethren.

24 fol. 65*b*. Love may be fatal. — Farhād, the sculptor-lover of Shīrīn, was beguiled to leap to death from the crag

when the old woman at the King's behest told him the false story of Shīrīn's death.

25 fol. 67*a*. Ḥāfiẓ and Fakhr ad-Dīn 'Abd aṣ-Ṣamad. — 'Trust Fate, and fear not the deceits of the beloved.'

26 fol. 72*b*. Ḥāfiẓ prefers wine to fasting as a means for cleansing the heart from sorrow.

27 fol. 76*b*. Fortune may come, just as Joseph, in spite of his brethren, attained to the pinnacle of success.

28 fol. 79*b*. Why be blamed, when Jamshīd and Kai Khusrau drank wine?

29 fol. 85*b*. Why be downcast? — 'The hoopoo, like the zephyr, may bring good tidings.' (The hoopoo bird was the messenger of love between Solomon and the Queen of Sheba. To be noted in the picture are the *dīvs*, or demons, as Solomon's servants.)

30 fol. 88*b*. My beloved is for me alone. — 'I would not touch King Solomon's seal if Abraham's hand had touched it.' (Again to be noted in the miniature are the *dīvs* as servants of Solomon, who is crowned with a nimbus.)

31 fol. 92*b*. Ḥāfiẓ realizes his hope.

32 fol. 93*b*. Love's mischances. — 'Lightning flashed from Lailā's tent and struck Majnūn's threshing-floor.'

33 fol. 97*a*. Ḥāfiẓ, like Iskandar (Alexander the Great), employs a mirror to find his beloved.

34 fol. 99*a*. 'All that you hold in your hand is air.'

35 fol. 100*a*. Lailā's burdened camel passing Majnūn's way.

36 fol. 105*a*. There may be risk in twos — two high domes, two Turks, two sailors, two mystics in a wine-house, two highwaymen, two lion-hunters, two seafarers, and two mischief-makers after Ḥāfiẓ's heart.

37 fol. 106*b*. ''Tis said the burden of the song in Jamshīd's company was this: "Bring wine, for Jamshīd will not live for ever." '

38 fol. 111*a*. Ḥāfiẓ complains of his beloved's inconstancy.

39 fol. 116*b*. Praise of Shāh Manṣūr Muẓaffar (d. 1392) for his victory over thousands.

40 fol. 118*a*. Ḥāfiẓ likens his beloved to his contemporary, the beneficent Shaikh Abū Isḥāq of Shīrāz (d. 1357), 'under whose feet the earth became a garden,'

and to Maḥmūd, 'the flash of whose eye burned up his enemies.'

41 fol. 122*a*. 'Few love stories stir us; they are those of Farhād and Shīrīn.'

42 fol. 128*b*. Ḥāfiẓ proposes to drink to the memory of Solomon's vizir Āsaf.

43 fol. 132*a*. 'O Lord, put into the heart of Khusrau and Shīrīn to be considerate of Farhād.'

44 fol. 142*a*. 'Not every polished face can catch the heart; not every mirror-maker knew Alexander's art.'

45 fol. 147*b*. Ḥāfiẓ gives to the east wind a message for kings about the charms of his beloved.

46 fol. 149*b*. On the transitoriness of love; it is passing.—'You may have the beautiful and brilliant turquoise seal of Abū Isḥāq (d. 1357), but his sway was short.'

47 fol. 159*b*. 'Set not your heart upon the world; ask the intoxicated about the virtue of the Cup and also about Jamshīd, the pleasure-seeker.'

48 fol. 162*a*. 'Despair not; for Joseph, though lost, will return again to Canaan, and his prison-cell will become a garden of roses.'

49 fol. 168*a*. Sulṭān Maḥmūd loved his favorite Ayāz simply for his beauty.

50 fol. 173*a*. 'If you aspire to sit as co-assessor of Khiḍr (who enjoyed eternal life at the Fountain of Youth) you must retire into concealment (as he did) from Alexander's eye.'

51 fol. 179*a*. 'Throw Bahrām's lasso around Jamshīd's cup, for in this Wilderness (of life) I see neither Bahrām nor his wild ass.'

52 fol. 183*a*. 'The turbaned Censor breaks the jar of wine.'

53 fol. 186*b*. Shāh Shujā' (1357–1384), the patron of Ḥāfiẓ.

54 fol. 196*a*. Yaḥyā ibn Muẓaffar (1353–1430), ruler of Shīrāz.

55 fol. 199*b*. Ḥāfiẓ in praise of Āsaf, the vizir of Solomon.

56 fol. 207*b*. Ḥāfiẓ praises Kai Qubād and Jamshīd.

57 fol. 210*b*. Manṣūr ibn Muḥammad of Shīrāz.

58 fol. 224*a*. Ḥāfiẓ praises the patience of Joseph.

59 fol. 229*b*. Ḥāfiẓ mentions Maḥmūd and his favorite Ayāz.

60 fol. 233*b*. Khwājah Tūrān Shāh (d. 1385), subject of Ḥāfiẓ's panegyric.

61 fol. 242*b*. Pashang's son, Afrāsiāb, a Tūrānian hero in the Shāh-nāmah.

62 fol. 245*a*. Farhād's death mentioned by Ḥāfiẓ.

63 fol. 250*a*. Shāh Shujā' (d. 1384).

64 fol. 260*b*. 'Give me Jamshīd's Cup and not the treasure of Qārūn.' (Qārūn of the Qur'ān, answering to Qorah of the Old Testament, represented the classic idea of Croesus and his wealth.)

65 fol. 263*b*. Joseph mentioned with praise.

66 fol. 265*b*. Nuṣrat ad-Dīn Yaḥyā, ruler of Shīrāz.

67 fol. 270*b*. Nuṣrat ad-Dīn Shāh Yaḥyā, above mentioned.

68 fol. 272*b*. 'To be king you must have the genius of Jamshīd and of Farīdūn; to be a lover like Majnūn you must follow the dangerous path of Lailā.'

69 fol. 277*b*. 'Many would be like Majnūn of the Tribe of Amīr, if a Lailā would come out of the Tribe of Ḥai.'

70 fol. 287*a*. The bountiful Ḥātim Ṭai.

71 fol. 294*a*. 'Whoever exchanged the treasure of economy for the treasure of the world, sold Joseph of Egypt cheap!'

72 fol. 298*b*. Muḥammad ibn 'Alī.

73 fol. 305*b*. Tūrān Shāh, mentioned above.

74 fol. 306*b*. 'Through this palace have passed a hundred thousand like Kā'ūs, Caesar, Jamshīd, and (other) kings.'

75 fol. 311*b*. 'As Majnūn followed the heart-ravishing Lailā, so my heart should follow its sweetheart.'

VII

JĀMĪ

JĀMĪ

(1414–1492 A.D.)

Jāmī, the last classic poet of Persia, is renowned for his historic, romantic, and mystic compositions. He took his name from his birthplace, the small town of Jām, near Herāt, in what is now called Afghānistān; yet he himself plays upon his name as emblematic of the 'cup,' *jām*, from which, with the mystic Ṣūfīs, he quaffed the divine love of God. See above, under Rūmī, p. 93.

Jāmī's seven longer poems are often collected together under the title *Haft Aurang*, or 'Seven Thrones,' after the name of the constellation of the Great Bear. A list of these poems is given below, in connection with the manuscripts. One among the number, and the best known, the *Yūsuf u Zulaikhā*, written in 1483 A.D., was probably inspired in title and subject by Firdausī's poem on the love of Potiphar's wife for Joseph; two others, namely the *Lailā u Majnūn* and the *Khirad-nāmah-i Iskandarī* go back to Niẓāmī's romantic poems by the same name, telling of Majnūn's tragic love and of Alexander's fame for wisdom. Jāmī's short lyric poems, which were composed approximately between 1460 and 1491, are later grouped in the manuscripts into three *dīwāns*. His prose work, *Bahāristān*, or 'Abode of Spring,' containing short stories with apt illustrations of Eastern thought and wisdom, was composed about 1487.

Jāmī traveled considerably during a part of his lifetime, making the pilgrimage to Mecca, and visiting Aleppo, Damascus, and other well-known cities, where he was received with the honor due to his literary attainments and with the recognition appropriate to his renown for mystic devotion. He died at Herāt in 1492.

For details and references consult, among other books, Ethé, *Neupersische Litteratur*, in *Grundriss*, 2. 305–307; S. Robinson, *Persian Poetry*, p. 510–642, London, 1883; F. H. Davis, *The Persian Mystics: II, Jāmī*, London, 1908; Jackson, art. 'Jāmī,' in C. D. Warner, *World's Best Literature*, 14. 8110–8116, New York, 1897.

17

Jāmī: Dīwān, an early collection of the lyric and mystic poems of Jāmī. This very valuable manuscript was written in the poet's own lifetime, as it can be assigned to the third quarter of the fifteenth century (see below), and it represents a compilation made prior to the time at which he grouped all of his lyric compositions into three *dīwāns*. The copy is in the handwriting of the celebrated calligraphist 'Abd al-Karīm of Khwārazm, whose brother transcribed, in 1463 A.D., another precious manuscript of Jāmī's Dīwān, which is most closely allied to this copy, and which is now in the British Museum (see below). Besides being richly illuminated, the present manuscript is adorned by sixteen beautiful miniatures, which show strongly the influence of Mongol art.

Size. — 10 × 6 in. (25.5 × 15.2 cm.); written space, $6\frac{3}{8} \times 3\frac{1}{8}$ in. (16.2 × 8.0 cm.). Folios 328; the last page is blank.

Binding. — Maroon Oriental leather, apparently camel's hide, deeply pressed with a medallion figure, pendants, and a panel border, gilded and with a tendril pattern in relief. The inside covers show a lighter brown leather, blind-pressed, and with elongated gold medallion, pendants, and corner angles, cut out and embellished by filigree work upon a blue background. The whole of the field is framed by a double gilt cording. The covers are the original ones, but have been slightly repaired.

Writing and Paper. — Written in a very beautiful Nasta'līq, 15 lines to a page in two columns, lightly outlined by gold ruling. The couplets in which Jāmī's name occurs in the poems are blocked off between horizontal ruled lines. The paper is of a heavy quality and of a creamish hue with a slight sheen.

Date and Scribe. — The date of the manuscript is not given, but can be determined, from the time of the scribe and from internal and external evidence, as being between 1463 and 1479 A.D., the former date being probably nearer the actual one. The determining factors as to the date are the following: —

The scribe gives his name in the colophon, on fol. 328*a*, as 'Abd al-Karīm of Khwārazm. This copyist, as we know through other sources, was one of the two noted sons of the famous calligraphist 'Abd ar-Raḥmān of Khwārazm, who flourished in Jāmī's own lifetime and enjoyed the patronage of Sulṭān Ya'qūb, ruler of the White Sheep Turkomans. The father and his two sons are accredited with having transformed, between the years 1456 and 1476, the style of Nasta'-līq writing (see Huart, *Les Calligraphes et les miniaturistes*, p. 257–258). As already stated, the other son was named 'Abd ar-Raḥīm, and he was the copyist who transcribed, in the year 1463 A.D., the similar early Dīwān of Jāmī, which is now in the British Museum (see Rieu, *Supplement*, p. 188, no. 288). The two copies by these celebrated brothers are closely related, although there are some differences between them. The British Museum manuscript has no preface, but the copy in the present collection has a preface (fol. 1*b*–5*b*), the close of which corresponds to what forms an epilogue at the end of the Museum copy, fol. 168 (see Rieu, *Supplement*, p. 189, for details regarding the latter). In a personal quatrain in the present preface (fol. 5*b*), moreover, Jāmī speaks of himself as being then in his fiftieth year, *i.e.* 1463 A.D.; exactly the same date is found in the epilogue (fol. 168) of the British Museum copy, the date of which is given as 1463. This year (1463) therefore forms the lower limit in determining the date of the manuscript. The upper limit is furnished either by the year 1476, when the transformation in the style of writing instituted by the father and his two sons was regarded as complete, as noted above; or it is given by 1479, the time when Jāmī began to revise or rearrange his poems into a form that ultimately became fixed as *Three Dīwāns* (cf. Ethé, *Neupersische Litteratur*, p. 306). The present copy, like the British Museum copy, antedates that event, and they resemble each other in agreeing largely in contents with what was later called the *First Dīwān*. It is not impossible that the two brothers Karīm and Raḥīm were engaged in making their respective transcripts almost at the same time.

Memorandums. — On the back of the binding, in a later Persian hand, is given the title with a note on the calligraphy, as 'The *Dīwān* of Jāmī, in beautiful handwriting.' On the first fly-leaf, which has been pasted together with the first folio, is a similar note, 'The *Dīwān* of Jāmī,' jotted by the same hand. To the right of this memorandum, in a different hand, there is a note erroneously calling the work by the name *Silsilat adh-Dhahab*, 'Chain of Gold,' as that is the title generally given to the first book of Jāmī's *Haft Aurang*. There are two small oval seals on this page, but they have been obliterated and are illegible. On the last fly-leaf is a pencil note in English regarding the author and possible date, as follows: 'Jami, Diwan, 1480–1500,' and a note as to the number of miniatures.

Subject and Arrangement. — An early Dīwān, or collection of Jāmī's lyric and mystic poems, made prior to the time when they were grouped as three separate dīwāns. As already remarked, this copy agrees largely in contents with what was later called the *First Dīwān* (cf. Sachau and Ethé, *Cat. Pers. Mss. Bodl. Lib.*, col. 612–614; also Muqtadir, *Cat. Arab. Pers. Mss.*, 2. 40–42; and especially Rieu, *Supplement*, p. 187–189, nos. 287, 288).

The arrangement, which is almost identical with that of the British Museum copy (Rieu, *Sup.*, no. 288), runs as follows: I. (*a*) A short personal *Preface* beginning in prose with موزون ترین کلامی (the same as in Rieu, p. 187, no. 287), then adding some verses in Maṣnawī form eulogizing the reigning sultan, Abū Sa'īd, furthermore continued by five lines of prose, and concluded by two quatrains (fol. 5*b*), in the first of which Jāmī states that he was then in the fiftieth (lunar) year of his age (*i.e.* 1463 A.D., see above). — (*b*) A group of five *Qaṣīdahs* in praise of God, followed by five *Tarjī'āt* in praise of Muḥammad, and by a succession of *Tarkīb-bands* and *Qaṣīdahs* (fol. 5*b*–39*a*); this whole latter group corresponds to what is generally called the second part (*b*) of the *First Dīwān*. — II. *Ghazals*, or odes, in alphabetical order (fol. 39*b*–291*b*). — III. *Tarjī'āt*, or poems with a refrain (fol. 291*b*–300*a*); the same as in Rieu, *Supplement*, no. 288. — IV. Two *Marsiyyahs* in Tarkīb-band form, one being an elegy on Maulānā Sa'd ad-Dīn of Kāshghar (d. 1455 A.D.), the other an elegy on Jāmī's own brother (fol. 300*b*–304*b*). — V. *Muqaṭṭa'āt*, fragmentary poems (fol. 304*b*–309*b*). — VI. *Rubā'iyāt*, or quatrains (fol. 309*b*–320*a*). — VIII. *Mu'ammayāt*, or enigmas, longer and shorter; the first of these (fol. 320*a*) is a riddle on the name of Shāh Bābar (d. 1457),[1] beginning در شهر دو جا, as in another copy of the Dīwān described by Rieu, *Sup.*, no. 288; the second enigma, also in four lines, on Ḥasan (fol. 320*b*); then seven other enigmas, each in two lines (fol. 321*b*), followed by a series of single-line (*fard*) riddles, the name

[1] This Bābar is the one called Bābar Sulṭān; he was the great-grandson of Tīmūr Lang, and after the death of 'Abd al-Laṭīf he established himself as ruler of Khurāsān in 1452, and died at Mashhad, on March 27, 1457; cf. Beale, *Oriental Biog. Dict.*, p. 92. He is to be distinguished from the later Bābar who founded the Mughal Dynasty.

of the person being given above each in a beautiful illuminated brooch (fol. 321*b*–328*a*).

Illuminations and Illustrations. — Two richly ornate full pages, in blue and gold, form the opening of the Preface; and there are throughout the manuscript, especially towards the end, highly decorated head-bands and caption-brooches. The miniatures, sixteen in all, many of them full-page, are fine specimens of art, strongly under the influence of the Mongol style; they appear to be the work of a single brush. The first two miniatures, occupying a double page before the two illuminated frontispieces, portray scenes of the chase; the other paintings, likewise often full-page, represent the subject of some particular verse or theme in the poem which they are chosen to illustrate. Details are as follows: —

1 fol. 1*b*.	Hunting-scene.
2 fol. 2*a*.	Another scene from the chase.
I (*a–b*) fol. 2*b*–3*a*.	Exquisite double title-pages in blue and gold.
3 fol. 21*a*.	'The young man who wishes to gain knowledge must dip deep like the diver to bring up the pearl.'
II (*c*) fol. 39*b*.	Illuminated title-piece to the book of Ghazals.
4 fol. 86*b*.	Convivial scene in spring, with a king sitting upon his throne in an orchard.
5 fol. 99*a*.	A bard playing on his guitar, for a prince and his company out of doors.
6 fol. 113*a*.	A feast of love.
7 fol. 132*a*.	'The student of thy love sets not his feet on the steps of the pulpit of the mosque.'
8 fol. 138*b*.	The shepherd takes Majnūn to the tent of Lailā, his beloved.
9 fol. 162*a*.	Illustration of a verse referring to Majnūn as devotedly following Lailā. The verse reads: 'When the camel-driver carries Lailā away from Ḥai, who can restrain Majnūn from following her?'
10 fol. 181*a*.	Illustration of Shīrīn and her sculptor-lover,

Farhād. The verse reads: 'My breast is shattered by the axe of thy love.'

11 fol. 202*a*. Spring scene — 'In the springtime, why give up the cup and social intercourse?'

12 fol. 218*b*. Scene of love-making — 'My love for thee has torn away the veil.'

13 fol. 228*a*. Polo scene — the lover chases his beloved like a polo ball.

14 fol. 232*a*. Hunting-scene — The beloved fears that her lover has come out to hunt her heart as in the chase.

15 fol. 263*b*. 'Seek thou for Jamshīd's Cup in the wine-glass, and for the water of life in the grape lees.'

16 fol. 284*b*. Jāmī would rather be the captive-game of his beloved than be a student.

18

Jāmī: Yūsuf and Zulaikhā. — A beautiful early sixteenth-century manuscript of Jāmī's romantic and mystic poem, *Yūsuf and Zulaikhā*. It is copied in the exquisite handwriting of the famous calligraphist Mīr 'Alī, and is dated 1523–1524 A.D. The illuminations, especially the sumptuous decoration of the margins, are particularly fine; and the three miniatures are in the style of the contemporary Bahzād school of painting. In its general style and character, it is to be closely associated with the great manuscript of Niẓāmī (No. 3) in the present collection, and it was finished one year earlier than that codex.

Size.—$10\frac{7}{8} \times 7$ in. (27.5×17.7 cm.); written surface, $5\frac{5}{8} \times 2\frac{5}{8}$ in. (14.3×6.7 cm.); the space covered by the writing is small in comparison with the wide margins. Folios 139, the first and last pages being blank, but especially embellished. A number of leaves are misbound, and some twelve in all are missing.

Binding. — Rebound in a heavy black Oriental leather, with blind-pressed designs in red, dark green, and gilt. Both the outside covers are alike, and show an inner field of black grained leather, set off by an inlaid red leather medallion, pendants, and corner angles, all these being stamped with a foliated pattern. The smaller panels around this field are of a dark green leather, with a similar pressed design, and a little gold and colored vignette at the top and the bottom heightens the effect. A running flowered border of gold serves to frame the whole. The inner covers are overlaid with a cloth of rich red color, with a floral pattern, but of ordinary quality.

Writing and Paper. — Written in an exquisite Nasta'līq hand by one of the most famous Persian calligraphists, Mīr 'Alī (see below). The text runs 14 lines to a page in two columns, separated by a double ruling and framed by a broad band of different colors, with floral traceries in gold. The whole page is then inset in a richly embellished wide margin, each border being painted in a different color from the next (thus giving the greatest variety) and being covered with gold flowered designs. The paper of the inset pages is of a heavy quality, but that of the borders is of a still heavier weight.

Date and Scribe. — Given in the colophon (fol. 137*a*) as, ' Written by Mīr 'Alī al-Ḥusainī, year nine hundred and thirty [*i.e.* 930 A.H. = 1523–1524 A.D.].' The name of this famous scribe is recorded also in a later memorandum on the first page (fol. 1*a*). Mīr 'Alī was the most celebrated penman of his day, and some idea of the value of his work may be gained from the statement of a European authority, R.

Murdock Smith, who mentions the fact of 'a single line of the writing of Mīr selling for two or three pounds sterling' (see Major R. M. Smith, *Persian Art*, p. 79, in *Handbooks of the South Kensington Museum*). Mīr 'Alī was indirectly, if not directly, the pupil of the renowned calligraphist Mashhadī. He was born at Herāt, but educated at Mashhad, and was later (1539) brought, much against his will, from Herāt to the court of the Uzbeg ruler at Bukhārā, where he was forced to employ his art of beautiful penmanship. He was also somewhat of a poet, and some verses, in which he laments his lot, have been preserved. He died in 1558 or 1559 A.D., or, according to another account, in 1544 A.D. (see Huart, *Les Calligraphes*, p. 227–228, and cf. Sachau and Ethé, *Cat. Pers. Mss. Bodl. Lib.*, nos. 816, 859, 863).

Memorandums. — The only memorandums are found on the first page (fol. 1*a*) and belong to a later date. At the top of this page is a note in Persian giving the title and author of the work as '*Yūsuf and Zulaikhā* by Jāmī.' In the middle of the page is a small oval modern seal containing the name of the owner, Faḍl Allāh, and the date 1324 A.H. = 1906 A.D. Above this seal is jotted, in a small neat hand, a memorandum stating that the manuscript 'was written by the renowned Mīr 'Alī, and was later acquired by Faḍl Allāh, of Rai, in the year 1326 A.H. [= 1908 A.D.].' (The difference between this date and the one preceding is, of course, in such a case a matter of no importance.) Rai is located about six miles southeast of Teherān.

Subject. — As already stated, the subject is the mystic and romantic poem of *Yūsuf and Zulaikhā*, or Joseph and Potiphar's wife, written by Jāmī in 1483 A.D., and dedicated to Sulṭān Ḥusain Mīrzā, ruler of Khurāsān, who resided at Herāt.

Illuminations and Illustrations. — Attention has been called above (under 'Writing') to the sumptuously illuminated margins and borders, and to the variety and alternation in the colors employed. There are two splendid 'unwāns to serve as a double frontispiece; and the head-bands, which form the captions to the different sections, are inscribed in rubric letters, set off by a tendril design in gold. The manuscript is illustrated by three full-page miniatures, which belong in style to the contemporary Bahzād school. No artist's name is given, but they are seemingly the work of a single painter, the last miniature (fol. 91*a*) being the finest of the three. The subjects are as follows: —

I (*a–b*)	fol. 1*b*–2*a*.	Two full-page introductory pieces, highly embellished.
1	fol. 58*b*.	Joseph arriving in Egypt and leaving the ship in the Nile.
2	fol. 69*a*.	Joseph tending the flocks.
3	fol. 91*a*.	Zulaikhā seizing the skirt of Joseph's robe.

19

Jāmī: Yūsuf and Zulaikhā, or the Story of Joseph and Potiphar's Wife. A fine Persian manuscript, not dated, but belonging to a period not later than the middle of the sixteenth century (see below), handsomely illuminated and containing four full-page miniature paintings after the best manner of the Bahzād school. Among its various owners were two of the Kings of Golkonda in Southern India.

Size. — 10 × $5\frac{3}{4}$ in. (25.3 × 14.6 cm.); written surface, $6\frac{5}{8}$ × 3 in. (16.8 × 7.5 cm.). Folios 162, the last page being blank; one leaf is missing after fol. 53, and one after fol. 78.

Embellished Introductory Page (ʿUnwān)
Ms. No. 18, fol. 2*a* (see page 148)

Binding. — Rebound in plain dark-red Oriental leather, with blue sheets tipped in opposite the illustrations. Some of the pages have been slightly repaired.

Writing and Paper. — Written in a beautiful Nasta'līq of a rather large size, 12 lines to a page in two gold-ruled columns, with orange, blue, and green outlines on tan-colored paper, gold-sprinkled, the pages being inset.

Date and Scribe. — The date is not given, but the manuscript may properly be assigned to the middle of the sixteenth century, or approximately to the year 1550 A.D., as may be judged not only from its general characteristics, but also from the time of the copyist. This scribe gives his name in the colophon as Muḥammad Qiwām of Shīrāz, and is the same person as the Muḥammad Qiwām of Shīrāz who, in August, 1556, finished copying a *Kulliyyāt* of Jāmī upon which he had worked for four years; he completed also in 1556 a beautiful transcript of Jāmī's *Yūsuf and Zulaikhā*; he is known also to have been the copyist of a manuscript of Jāmī's *Haft Aurang* (see Sachau and Ethé, *Catalogue of Persian Manuscripts in the Bodleian Library*, nos. 895, 898, 905); see also next paragraph.

Memorandums. — The copy contains a number of seals together with some memorandums. On the back of the title-page (fol. 1*a*) are half a dozen signets, the oldest of which is apparently the small oval seal near the bottom and at the top, again repeated on the last folio; it is the signet of one Riḍā, who terms himself 'the humble servant of the descendants of Muḥammad.' Near it is a Persian memorandum which records: 'This (book) was brought by the Dervish Beg on the 7th of the blessed month of Ramaḍān in the year Alf (1000) from Dār-maḥal [District Library?].' The reckoning of the year Alf, 'Millennium,' was introduced by Akbar the Great, and was counted, not from the flight

(Hijra) of Muḥammad in 622 A.D., but from his death, which occurred in 632 A.D. The date of the memorandum would correspond to Sept. 25, 1582. The small oblong seal in the middle of the same page (fol. 1*a*) is the signet, with date, of 'Zain al-'Ābidīn, year 1190 A.H. [= 1776 A.D.].' Above it is a large round seal with a crest, bearing the name of Sulṭān Muḥammad, one of the rulers of the later Qutb Shāh dynasty of Golkonda in Southern India, together with the date 1210 A.H. = 1795 A.D. A small seal near the edge, but partly clipped off, is the same as one on the last folio and can be read as that of 'Mahdī Qulī, the servant of Shāh Ḥamzah.' The three other oblong seals on fol. 1*a* are obliterated. On the first fly-leaf is the large seal of Muḥammad Qulī, who was another of the Qutb Shāhs of Golkonda. A small square seal near the top is obliterated, but below it is written in Persian in a bold hand: 'With the acknowledgment of Mīr Kāẓim, on the sixth of Ramaḍān, in the year 1122 A.H. [= Oct. 29, 1710 A.D.].' The two seals on the last folio have already been described.

Subject and Contents. — Jāmī's poem on the story of the love of Potiphar's wife for Joseph, comprising approximately 3544 rimed couplets.

Illuminations and Illustrations. — The manuscript is introduced by two beautiful 'unwāns, that form a double title-page, and contain, in medallions, the opening couplets of the book *Yūsuf and Zulaikhā*. In addition to these there are throughout the poem, as captions to the different sections, large gold bands, lettered in white and delicately flowered. There are four highly finished miniature paintings, of the most delicate workmanship, the portrait of Joseph being recognizable in each case by a painted golden nimbus. They furnish fine examples of the art of the Ṣafavid period. The subjects of the illustrations are as follows: —

I (*a–b*) fol. 1*b*–2*a*. Illuminated double introductory pages.

1 fol. 38*a*. Zulaikhā with her handmaidens in the palace, after she has dreamed of Yūsuf the second time.

2 fol. 73*a*. Yūsuf, offered for sale, is purchased by Zulaikhā for double the price bid.

3 fol. 102*b*. Yūsuf summoned by Zulaikhā to serve at feast. The Egyptian ladies who are present are so overcome by his beauty that they cut their fingers instead of cutting the pomegranates they are peeling.

4 fol. 139*b*. Yūsuf and Zulaikhā united in wedlock after Potiphar's death.

20

Jāmī: Haft Aurang, or 'Seven Thrones,' named after the constellation of the Great Bear. An illuminated manuscript of about the middle of the eighteenth century, containing Jāmī's seven longer poems complete, and illustrated by seventeen miniatures.

Size. — $11\frac{3}{4} \times 7\frac{1}{4}$ in. (29.7 × 18.5 cm.); written surface, $7\frac{7}{8} \times 4\frac{5}{8}$ in. (20.0 × 11.8 cm.); folios 257, numbered in Persian figures. Between each of the seven poems the scribe has left blank a page, or, in some cases, two pages.

Binding. — Strong modern Persian binding of dark brown calf; the covers are blind-pressed and slightly gilded; the stitching of the head-band is in Shīrāzī style.

Writing and Paper. — Fair and clear Nasta'līq, 21 lines to a page, in four columns, separated by gold rulings and framed in gold and blue lines. The paper is of ordinary weight, creamish in hue, and without sheen. Small gilt paper tabs are added on the margin of the pages that have miniatures and illuminations.

Date and Scribe. — The date is not given and the scribe does not add his name; but the date must be about the middle of the eighteenth century A.D., if we may judge from a Persian memorandum on the first page and on the last page containing the year 1178 A.H. = 1764 A.D. (see below).

Memorandums. — On the outer margin near the top of the first page (fol. 1*a*) is a memorandum in Persian by the owner, over his (later effaced) seal, as follows: 'My courteous and sincere friend Āqā Muḥammad Rabī' Ṣāḥib (may the peace of God be upon him!) granted (this book) to me in the month of Jumāda al-Awwal . . . .' The year is erased, but was probably 1178 A.H. = 1764 A.D., as below. In another hand underneath this seal, and again near the top of the page, is '450' (*i.e.* 450 tūmāns, as value). Practically the same memorandum over the same seal (likewise effaced), but in another hand, is found near the bottom of the last page (fol. 257*b*), namely: 'Āqā Muḥammad Rabī' Ṣāḥib (may the peace of God be upon him!) presented (this book) to me as an offering and gift in the month of Jumāda al-Awwal, year 1178 A.H. [= October, 1764 A.D.],' and the number '450' is added by the *tertia manus* that placed those figures twice on the opening page to denote the value. The seal is identical with that at the opening, but, as stated, it has been erased; a seal nearby has also been obliterated. A Persian memorandum at the top of fol. 1*a* notes that the book is 'the seven (poems) of Jāmī complete.' In the decoration on the upper left-hand corner of this first page is the number '257 folios,' referring correctly to the number of leaves contained in the manuscript. On fol. 66*a*, which is blank, there is a large octagonal seal, apparently of a person of high rank, but it is defaced and can be only partially deciphered as the signet of 'Muḥammad Farrukh Mīr . . . Zain al-'Ābidīn. . . .' On a fly-leaf tipped in near the beginning of the book is a Persian memorandum giving the names of the seven books of Jāmī contained in the manuscript. All the other memorandums on the fly-leaves are in English, fly-leaf 4 giving a table of contents and a list of the illustrations, and fly-leaf 7 giving a similar enumeration of the seven poems contained in the copy, together with a memorandum as to the Persian jotting translated above. The same English hand has noted on, the margins opposite the miniatures the subjects they illustrate.

Subject and Arrangement. — The *Haft Aurang*, or Seven Thrones, of Jāmī, arranged as follows: I. *Silsilat adh-Dhahab*, fol. 1*b*–50*a*. — II. *Salāmān u Absāl*, fol. 51*b*–65*b*. — III. *Tuḥfat al-Aḥrār*, fol. 66*b*–88*b*. — IV. *Subḥat al-Abrār*, fol. 89*b*–126*b*. — V. *Yūsuf u Zulaikhā*, fol. 127*b*–177*b*. — VI. *Lailā u Majnūn*, fol. 178*b*–226*a*. — VII. *Khirad-nāmah-i Iskandarī*, fol. 227*b*–257*b*.

Illuminations and Illustrations. — There are seven illuminated 'unwāns as title-pieces to the seven books, and there is also an ornate medallion page in colors as an opening to the work (fol. 1*a*). The captions to the various sections in the different poems are written alternately in gold and in red. One special page (fol. 43*a*) which contains a reference to Majnūn's freeing a deer from a hunter because of his love for Lailā is extra-illuminated with gold interlineations and an ornate floral border. The miniatures in this manuscript are seventeen in number and appear to be by three or four different artists in the general style of the period; that on fol. 171*a* seems to show traces of Indian influence, which is not the case with the others.

I (*a*) fol. 1*a*. Ornamental medallion page.
(*b*) fol. 1*b*. Illuminated title-piece to the *Silsilat adh-Dhahab*.

	1	fol. 29*a*.	Zāhid knocks at the door of his sweetheart as she is entertaining 'Ārif.
	2	fol. 37*a*.	The wicked man and the woman with the two skins filled with melted butter.
II	(*c*)	fol. 51*b*.	Illuminated title-piece to *Salāmān and Absāl*.
	3	fol. 58*a*.	Salāmān and Absāl playing polo.
III	(*d*)	fol. 66*b*.	Illuminated title-piece to *Tuḥfat al-Aḥrār*.
IV	(*e*)	fol. 89*b*.	Illuminated title-piece to *Subḥat al-Abrār*.
V	(*f*)	fol. 127*b*.	Illuminated title-piece to *Yūsuf and Zulaikhā*.
	4	fol. 137*a*.	Zulaikhā dreams of Joseph and afterwards tells her attendants the story of her love.
	5	fol. 153*b*.	In order to tempt Joseph, Zulaikhā enthrones him in a beautiful garden and surrounds him with fair damsels.
	6	fol. 161*a*.	The Egyptian ladies, overcome by Joseph's beauty, cut their fingers instead of the pomegranates which they are peeling.
	7	fol. 171*a*.	Joseph marries Zulaikhā after Potiphar's death.
VI	(*g*)	fol. 178*b*.	Illuminated title-piece to *Lailā and Majnūn*.
	8	fol. 197*b*.	King Naufal while out hunting sees the love-distracted Majnūn and takes pity upon him.
	9	fol. 204*b*.	The Caliph sends for Majnūn, who comes into his presence.
	10	fol. 209*b*.	Majnūn becomes a hermit in the wilderness after hearing of Lailā's marriage.
	11	fol. 217*b*.	Lailā pays a visit to Majnūn in the desert.
	12	fol. 224*a*.	Lailā's coffin is carried to burial.
VII	(*h*)	fol. 227*b*.	Illuminated title-piece to *Khirad-nāmah-i Iskandarī*, or Book of Alexander.
	13	fol. 243*b*.	Iskandar, or Alexander the Great, and his Court.
	14	fol. 241*b*.	Alexander and the foolish sage.
	15	fol. 243*a*.	Alexander destroying an idol-temple.
	16	fol. 248*b*.	The sage alone is saved when the boat is wrecked, as he lets everything go.
	17	fol. 253*b*.	Death of Alexander.

TURKISH MANUSCRIPTS

ORNATE LACQUER BINDING

Ms. No. 21, outside of cover (see page 160)

VIII

MĪR 'ALĪ SHĪR NAWĀ'Ī

MĪR 'ALĪ SHĪR NAWĀ'Ī

(1441–1501 A.D.)

Mīr 'Alī Shīr Nawā'ī, or Nawā'ī for short, a distinguished poet and eminent man of affairs, was born at Herāt, February 9, 1441 (17 Ramaḍān, 844 A.H.), studied at Mashhad and at Samarqand, and then returned to his native city, where honored preferment awaited him at the court of the ruling sultan, Ḥusain ibn Bāiqarā, to whom he became grand vizir. Among the high offices of trust which he discharged was that of Secretary of Finance, and, for a year, the Governorship of Jurjān, on the Caspian Sea. His own preference, however, was for private life, into which he finally withdrew, employing his large wealth in the patronage of letters and in charity, as well as devoting himself to writing poetry, an occupation that appears to have been ever nearest to his heart.

Nawā'ī's poetical works in Jaghatā'ī, or Eastern Turkish, entitle him to the foremost rank among Turkish writers, although he was an equal master of verse in Persian as well. The first collection of his youthful compositions appears to have been made by his admiring friend Prince Muḥammad Sulṭān, who died in 1484 A.D. (889 A.H.), and his works in all comprise nine volumes of verse and twelve of prose. His lyric poems show strongly the influence of Ḥāfiẓ. Nawā'ī's death occurred in his sixtieth year at Herāt, 12 Jumāda II, 906 A.H. = Jan. 3, 1501 A.D.

Consult Rieu, *Catalogue of the Turkish Manuscripts in the British Museum*, p. 273, London, 1888; Rieu, *Cat. Pers. Mss. Brit. Mus.*, 1. 366; and especially Gibbs, *History of Ottoman Poetry*, 1. 127–129, et passim; compare also Berezin, *Beschreibung der türkisch-tatarischen Handschriften in den Petersburger Bibliotheken*, in *Zt. d. deutsch. Morgenländischen Gesellschaft*, 2. 248–256, Leipzig, 1848; Belin, *Notice sur Mir Ali-Chîr-Névâïi*, in *Journal Asiatique*, cinquième série, 17 (1861), p. 175–256, 281–357.

21

Mīr ʻAlī Shīr Nawā'ī: A Dīwān. This very valuable manuscript, dated 1499–1500 A.D., contains a collection of lyric poems in Jaghatā'ī, or Eastern Turkish, by Nawā'ī, and was copied during the author's own lifetime, a year or two before his death, by the famous calligraphist ʻAlī Mashhadī, his special protégé. The manuscript is richly illuminated and has fifteen miniatures besides the two lacquer paintings on the inside of the covers.

Size. — $9\frac{1}{2} \times 6$ in. (24×15.1 cm.); written surface, $7\frac{1}{4} \times 4$ in. (19.2×10.4 cm.). Folios 254, the first and the last leaf blank; a folio is missing after each of the following: fol. 108, 148, 183, 226, and 250.

Binding. — Ornate lacquer binding with lacquer paintings on the inside of the covers, the manuscript having probably been rebound about the end of the sixteenth century. The field of both of the outer covers is identical and has a foliated design, chiefly of a golden yellow color, with a sort of cruciform medallion set off by pendants of black and gold, the entire panel being then framed by a triple border of black, red, and black, ornamented by a running flower pattern. The inside of the front cover (*a*) has a lacquer painting presenting a scene at the court of a ruler before whom an old woman makes a petition; the inner back cover (*b*) gives in lacquer a scene at an academy of learning. The details in both of these pictures are well worthy of observation. When the manuscript was rebound (as already noted), the edges of the folios were slightly trimmed and then gilded.

Writing and Paper. — Exquisite Nastaʻlīq by the hand of the famous ʻAlī Mashhadī; the writing runs 15 lines to a page

Lacquer Painting on a Manuscript Cover
Ms. No. 21, inside of back cover (see page 160)

in two columns separated by double rulings of gold, and heavily bordered by lines of blue, gold, orange, and red. The paper is a fairly light laid paper of regular texture and a comparatively high finish, with somewhat of an ivory shade, the written part of the page being dusted with gold so as to lend additional elegance to the copy.

Date and Scribe. — Both the name of the scribe and the date of the manuscript are given in the colophon, which runs as follows: 'Written by the poor Sulṭān 'Alī al-Mashhadī (may his sins be forgiven!) in the year nine hundred and five [905 A.H. = 1499–1500 A.D.] at the capital, Herāt.'

'Alī Mashhadī, who was called 'Sulṭān' from his mastery of penmanship, is acknowledged to have brought the art of Nasta'līq handwriting to its highest perfection, and he enjoyed the special favor and protection of Nawā'ī as a patron. He is known to have co-operated with the famous miniaturist Bahzād in preparing a royal manuscript of the History of Tamerlane, which formed a part of the collection of works in the library of the Mughal Emperor Humāyūn and which afterwards passed into the possession of Akbar the Great. Mashhadī's death occurred in 1513 A.D., and he was buried in his birthplace, the city of Mashhad. For further details regarding him see Huart, *Les Calligraphes et les miniaturistes de l'Orient musulman*, p. 221–222; likewise Sarre and Martin, *Meisterwerke Muhammedanischer Kunst*, 1. plates 23, 31, Munich, 1912.

Memorandums. — On the first page is a Persian memorandum giving the title of the book and noting that it is composed in Turkish. On fol. 28*a* is another Persian memorandum in badly faded ink, saying: 'This book is the property of Muḥammad Nūyān; any one that steals or sells it will be arrested.' The miniatures have been numbered later in Persian figures on the margins.

Subject and Arrangement. — A Dīwān of Nawā'ī, containing a collection of more than eight hundred ghazals, or odes, together with some other short poems, gathered into a group one or two years before his death, and arranged as follows: I. *Ghazals* (816 in number; 53 of which rime in Alif), fol. 3*b*–234*b*. — II. *Badā'i'* verses, or cunning odes (five in number), fol. 234*b*–237*a*. — III. *Tarjī'āt*, or poems with a refrain, fol. 237*a*–250*b*. — IV. *Rubā'īs*, or quatrains (33 in number), together with three hemistich *Fards*, fol. 250*b*–254*a*.[1]

Illuminations and Illustrations. — The two front pages are occupied by full-sized illuminations of elaborate design. There are ornate caption-bands to each of the eight hundred and more odes contained in the book. All the pages are gold-besprinkled, and those opposite the miniatures are richly set off by gold interlineations, which are added likewise in the text above and below the paintings. Besides the two illustrations on the inside of the lacquer covers, described above under 'Binding,' there are fifteen fine miniatures to illustrate the text. These miniatures are nearly of full-page size, and they show in style the high art of the Herāt school at the time. They are all the work of one artist, but no name is given. Their subjects are conventional, chosen to match the special theme of the ode that is illustrated. The portrait of the king who is represented is the same throughout, with the exception of fol. 2*b*, 17*b*, 125*a*, 209*b*. It is possible to conjecture that the younger ruler represents Sulṭān Husain Bāiqarā, the Tīmūrid

[1] This manuscript bears no special title-heading to show which of the four dīwāns it is, into which the poems were finally grouped before the poet's death, and it has no preface, but it has the same beginning as one of the dīwāns of Nawā'ī in the British Museum (Add. 7910) described by Rieu, *Cat. Turkish Mss. Brit. Mus.*, Add. 7910, p. 296, London, 1888, the opening of the first ghazal in both copies being, زهی ظهور جمالینك قویاش كیبی پیدا

monarch of Khurāsān, to whom Nawāʾī was minister. His royal consort was Khadījah Begüm Āqā; possibly she is represented, as indicated, in four of the miniatures noted below. The elder king (four times represented) may possibly be Ḥusain's father, Manṣūr. These miniatures, in addition to the lacquer paintings, are as follows:—

I	(*a–b*)	fol. 1*b*–2*a*.	Two full pages illuminated as frontispieces.
	1	fol. 2*b*.	A king pronouncing sentence; his son is standing near him.
	2	fol. 3*a*.	Convivial scene in a king's harem.
	(*c*)	fol. 3*b*.	Illuminated head-piece to the collection of poems.
	3	fol. 17*b*.	A king with his attendants by a stream in a garden.
	4	fol. 27*b*.	The king and his consort enjoying music in a garden.
	5	fol. 51*a*.	The king listening to a court poet.
	6	fol. 74*a*.	The king seated beneath a tree and about to partake of wine.
	7	fol. 85*a*.	A scene in the king's royal chamber.
	8	fol. 108*a*.	The king and his consort under a pavilion out of doors.
	9	fol. 125*a*.	A king under a pavilion surrounded by his courtiers.
	10	fol. 141*b*.	The king out riding meets with his consort and her handmaiden on horseback.
	11	fol. 153*b*.	The king and his son listening to women musicians.
	12	fol. 171*a*.	A levee by the king under the trees.
	13	fol. 209*b*.	Female musicians playing before a king and his consort in their tent.
III	14	fol. 237*b*.	The cupbearer hands wine to the king.
	15	fol. 245*a*.	The king giving orders to his officers of state.

22

Mīr 'Alī Shīr Nawā'ī: Second Dīwān, entitled *Nawādir ash-Shabāb*, or 'The Choice Things of Youth.' This manuscript, belonging to the last quarter of the sixteenth century (being dated 1580 A.D.), and written in Jaghatā'ī, or Eastern Turkish, contains a collection of ghazals, or odes, and other short poems, by Nawā'ī; it is ornately illuminated and is adorned by five full-page miniatures, two of them occupying the front and the last page respectively.

Size. — $10\frac{3}{4} \times 7$ in. (27.3×17.8 cm.); written surface, $6\frac{7}{8} \times 4$ in. (17.6×10.2 cm.). Folios 224; a folio is missing after fol. 77, 133, 169; not however after fol. 201, where the catchword is erroneously taken from the second line of the next page, instead of from the first line.

Binding. — Rebound in the original Persian flap-covers of dark leather embellished by designs after the style of the period. Both covers are identical in model. The pattern and colors are best preserved on the flap, which coincides precisely with the covers in design, and shows a panel of pressed black leather with gold stamping and tendril pattern, surrounding a central medallion of blue, orange, and green, forming a pendulum between two corresponding smaller pendants above and below, offset again by decorative angles at the corners of the field. The whole is bordered by a framework of panel-bands, all of which, like the other patterns, exhibit the remains of filigree work finely cut out of the leather, even though the tooling is less skilfully done than in some of the bindings already described. The inner cover is overspread with a plain red leather, such as is often used in Persian bindings, and has the stitching of the two headbands done in the style called Shīrāzī.

Writing and Paper. — The writing is a medium-sized Nasta'līq, by a beautiful hand, 14 lines to a page in two columns separated by a heavy bar of gold and green with a running flower design in black; the border lines that surround the written surface are of green, orange, gold, white, and blue. The paper, tinted a dull pink color, is of a laid base and is somewhat uneven in composition; in some cases the laid marks are hardly distinguishable.

Date and Scribe. — The date in the colophon (where the title is repeated as *Nawādir ash-Shabāb*, or 'Second Dīwān') is fully written out in words as 'nine hundred and eighty-eight,' *i.e.* 988 A.H. = 1580 A.D. The scribe's name is added as 'Qāsim 'Alī of Shīrāz.'

Memorandums. — There are two small oval seals stamped on fol. 224*a*; one is that of a person named Mūsā, but the other has been partly destroyed in rebinding and cannot be deciphered. There are no memorandums except some unimportant pencil jottings of numbers recently made on the last fly-leaf, and some marginal notes, in ink, of the Persian equivalents for Turkish words on fol. 141*a*, 141*b*, 142*b*.

Subject and Arrangement. — I. *Ghazals*, or odes, about six hundred in number (37 of them riming in Alif), fol. 1*b*–192*a*. — II. *Mustazād*, or distichs with a supplement, fol. 192*a*–193*a*. — III. *Mukhammas*, or quintuple verses, fol. 193*a*–197*a*. — IV. *Sāqī-nāmah*, a book of verses on wine, fol. 197*a*–201*a*. — V. *Maṣnawīs*, or rimed couplets, 201*a*–206*b*. — VI. *Muqaṭṭa'āt*, or miscellaneous short fragments, 206*b*–213*a*. — VII. *Rubā'iyāt*, or quatrains, 213*a*–224*a*.

Illuminations and Illustrations. — The manuscript is sumptuously illuminated. Besides the embellished frontispiece and a half dozen smaller title-bands, there are also two ornamental framework designs with floweret wreaths at the beginning of each of the six hundred odes; there are likewise similar ornamental triangles adorning the entire series of quatrains. A heavy interlineation of gold embellishes the page opposite each miniature. The miniatures themselves are apparently the work of a single artist, of the Ṣafavid period, but not named; and in subject they represent themes referred to in the odes..

	1	fol. 1*a*.	Out-of-door scene with preparation being made for a noon-day meal.
I	(*a*)	fol. 1*b*.	Illuminated title-piece to the *Ghazals*.
	2	fol. 15*b*.	A contest of skill in archery on horseback.
	3	fol. 59*b*.	Hunting-scene.
	4	fol. 186*b*.	A tournament at arms.
VII	5	fol. 224*b*.	A scene of conviviality at court.

ARABIC MANUSCRIPTS

IX

QUR'ĀN

QUR'ĀN

The sacred book of the Muḥammadan religion, containing the utterances of the Prophet as a direct revelation from Allāh through the angel Gabriel. These varied discourses, extending over a period of more than twenty years down to Muḥammad's death in 632 A.D., are comprised in 114 chapters, called *sūrahs,* of different lengths; and they are arranged in general according to the length, the longest first and the shortest last, and not according to the subject-matter or the time of their utterance. Earliest in the point of time are the sūrahs delivered at Mecca, between 610 and 622 A.D.; those which were delivered at Medīna, after the Flight (Hijra) in 622 A.D., form a later group.

The contents of the Qur'ān may briefly be summarized as comprising Muḥammad's teachings regarding the unity of God and the divine nature of the prophetic mission, the doctrine of a future life, heaven and hell, other special tenets of the faith and rites to be observed by true believers, together with much narrative material of a didactic character drawn from antiquity.

The earliest redaction of the work as a sacred book was made in 633 A.D., a year after Muḥammad's death, by his secretary, Zaid ibn Ṣābit, at the command of the Caliph Abū Bakr. A second redaction was made nearly twenty years later, in 650 A.D., under the supervision of the same scribe, at the bidding of the Caliph Oṣmān; and this became the recognized standard of the canon.

The veneration in which the Qur'ān is held led naturally to the bestowal of the greatest care and lavish expense on the preparation of copies of the text. Religious merit was believed to accrue to one who transcribed a manuscript of it; and even kings and princes showed their religious devotion by accomplishing the task, as in the case of the manuscript described below.

23-24

Qur'ān. — A very beautiful and interesting copy of the Qur'ān bound in two volumes and bearing the date Fourth of Ramaḍān 830 A.H. = June 29, 1427 A.D. The manuscript is especially valuable because it was copied by the hand of Ibrāhīm Sulṭān, the grandson of Tamerlane, and passed down through the line of the Great Mughal Rulers, as it contains a long memorandum (given below), which was made more than two centuries later, on the back of the last folio, by the Emperor Aurangzīb, then a prince in his twentieth year, thus showing that he also personally used this copy.

Size.—8 × 5½ in. (20.3 × 14.0 cm.); written surface, 5⅜ × 3¼ in. (13.7 × 8.7 cm.). Folios: in the first volume, 267 folios; in the second volume, 268 folios. This latter volume begins five verses before the end of Sūrah 18, entitled The Cave.

Binding. — Rebound in old Oriental leather covers of a maroon color, with medallion and pendants blind-pressed, but with no special ornamentation.

Writing and Paper. — The writing is a very elegant Naskhī hand which does full credit to its princely copyist; and the text is vocalized throughout. It runs 10 lines to a page and is inclosed by gold, orange, and blue rulings. The blackness of the ink is made the more noticeable by the rich gilding between the lines, while all the chapter-titles are written in a blue ink, the last few alternating with gold. The punctuation between the verses is marked by a large gold period. There are also numerous rubrics both in the body of the text and on the margins, as well as marginal annotations in black by different hands. These annotations, of a critical and technical nature, were probably added by scholars at the court of Shāh Rukh, the father of Sulṭān Ibrāhīm Mīrzā, after the prince had finished copying

A KING LISTENING TO A COURT POET
Ms. No. 21, fol. 51*a* (see page 163)

the book, because the illuminations on the borders were painted after the notes were made, as is proved by the careful manner in which they are traced to avoid interfering with the writing.[1]

The paper in both volumes is of the same quality, medium in weight, and has a dull finish; its texture has become slightly brittle with the lapse of time. The fly-leaves are of a later date and belong to the time when the two volumes were rebound.

Date and Scribe. — Both are given in the colophon in the second volume (vol. 2, fol. 267*a*), the date of the completion being Ramaḍān 4, 830 A.H. = June 29, 1427. The scribe, as already stated, was a grandson of Tamerlane and son of Shāh Rukh, and gives his name in full as Ibrāhīm Sulṭān bin Shāh Rukh bin Tīmūr Gūrgān. This Ibrāhīm Sulṭān was a renowned patron of letters, and under his personal supervision was prepared the well-known history of his grandfather's achievements, entitled the *Ẓafar-nāmah*, or 'Book of Tamerlane's Victories,' which was compiled by his teacher Sharaf ad-Dīn 'Alī Yazdī. Ibrāhīm was famous for his six different styles of handwriting, and it is related that a specimen of his penmanship which he purposely signed with the name of a famous calligraphist, whose style he could imitate, was so perfect that it was taken

[1] The nature of these annotations is masoretic; they consist of comments on the orthography of the text, variant readings, and the pauses to be observed in reciting it; they are often marked with a letter to denote the particular Reader (*Qārī*) or Traditionist (*Rāwī*) upon whose authority they are based. A list of these ten Readers and twenty Traditionists is given on the last folio (fol. 268*a*) of the second volume (compare also Nöldeke, *Geschichte des Qoran's*, pp. 287–298, Göttingen, 1860). The Thirty Divisions (*Ajzā'*) and the Sixty Subdivisions (*Aḥzāb*), into which the Qur'ān is divided for convenience in recitation, are regularly indicated on the margin in red letters. The names of the Sūrahs are marked in black ink in a minuscule hand on the upper left-hand corner of the folios.

for an original and was sold in the market-place for a very high price. He died in 1430 or 1431 A.D., about six years after he finished transcribing the present manuscript; see also Huart, *Les Calligraphes et les miniaturistes*, p. 96–97; and compare Elliot, *History of India*, 3. 391.

Memorandums. — As already noted, there is, on the back of the last folio of the second volume, a memorandum which is of the greatest interest and value, as it is by the hand of the Mughal Emperor Aurangzīb, then a prince in his twentieth year, or more than two centuries after the manuscript was written. It is in Arabic, as suited to the language of the Qur'ān, though in the Persian style of handwriting; and one of the court artists has gilded the page around it. The memorandum reads verbatim as follows: —

'God the Most High.
In His Name — Praise be to Him.

This Excellent Book and Discourse, which speaks the truth, namely the Venerated Qur'ān, the Exalted Scripture, in the handwriting of the grandson of the greatest of the sultans of time and the sublimest of the kings of the ages [*i.e.* in the handwriting of Tamerlane's grandson], Sulṭān Ibrāhīm, son of Mīrzā Shāh Rukh, son of Amīr Tīmūr Ṣāḥib Qirān [1] — (may [God] cause them to dwell in the highest gardens of Paradise!) — which book has been intrusted to me, and the keeping of it is an obligation upon me. I — who rely upon the assurance of His universal grace and upon the intercession of His Prophet, when He shall resuscitate the bones and rebuild (?) the body (?) — am Aurangzīb, the son of the sultan of sultans and most just king of kings, Shihāb ad-Dīn Muḥammad Ṣāḥib Qirān the Second, Shāh Jahān the Victorious Emperor,[2] may his kingdom and empire be everlasting! In the months of the year one thousand and forty-

[1] These last four words, giving Tamerlane's name as a help towards understanding the long titles, are added by Aurangzīb himself in the margin.

[2] Aurangzīb adds in the margin the words 'Shāh Jahān the Victorious Emperor' so as to make clearer the application of the long titles in his memorandum.

eight from the Flight of the Prophet [*i.e.* 1048 A.H. = 1638–1639 A.D.]. Upon its Lord be most copious blessings and benedictions!'

The only other memorandum is of a later date; it is on the last fly-leaf and consists of two lines of a prayer in Arabic invoking the blessing of God.

Subject. — The Qur'ān, or Sacred Book of Islām, complete in one hundred and fourteen Sūrahs (chapters). Appended after the colophon, and still in the same hand of Sulṭān Ibrāhīm, is a prayer in eleven lines (found also in other copies of the Qur'ān) to be repeated after reading the sacred book; it begins, 'O Allāh, benefit and uplift me, etc.' Following this, in a different hand, but with illumination around it, is the brief list of the ten 'Readers' and twenty 'Traditionists,' as explained in a previous footnote.

Illuminations. — The manuscript is ornately illuminated with two introductory medallions (described below), three rich title-pieces, and with highly decorated borders. These borders have delicate foliated designs painted in gold; and thirty-one of them have extra adornment consisting of a very artistic flowered pattern traced in different colors upon a background of gold. The main details as to the illuminations are as follows: —

(*a–b*) fol. 1*b*–2*a*. Two octagonal rosette medallions illuminated with gold and blue designs and centered in the midst of foliated ornamentations which are similar to the general decorations of the borders throughout the manuscript. Within these medallions is inscribed, in white ink, the following appropriate quotation from the Qur'ān itself (17. 90): 'If mankind and the genii came together to produce the like of this Qur'ān, they could not produce its like, even though the one of them should assist the other.'

(*c–d*) fol. 2*b*–3*a*. Two illuminated full-page titles including the opening Sūrah of the Qur'ān.

(*e*) fol. 3*b*. Illuminated title-piece for the second Sūrah.

Thirty-one extra-illuminated borders, mentioned above; these are found at the places marking the majority of the Divisions, called Aḥzāb; they are mostly in pairs on opposite pages, and occur on the following folios: First volume, fol. 19*b*, 20*a*, 54*b*, 55*a*, 90*b*, 91*a*, 143*b*, 144*a*, 178*b*, 179*a*, 213*b*, 214*a*, 247*b*, 248*a*.—Second volume, fol. 16*b*, 17*a*, 50*b*, 51*a*, 85*b*, 86*a*, 120*a*, 121*b*, 155*b*, 156*a*, 191*b*, 225*a*, 228*b*, 266*b*, 267*a*, 267*b* (Prayer), 268*a* (List of Readers and Traditionists).

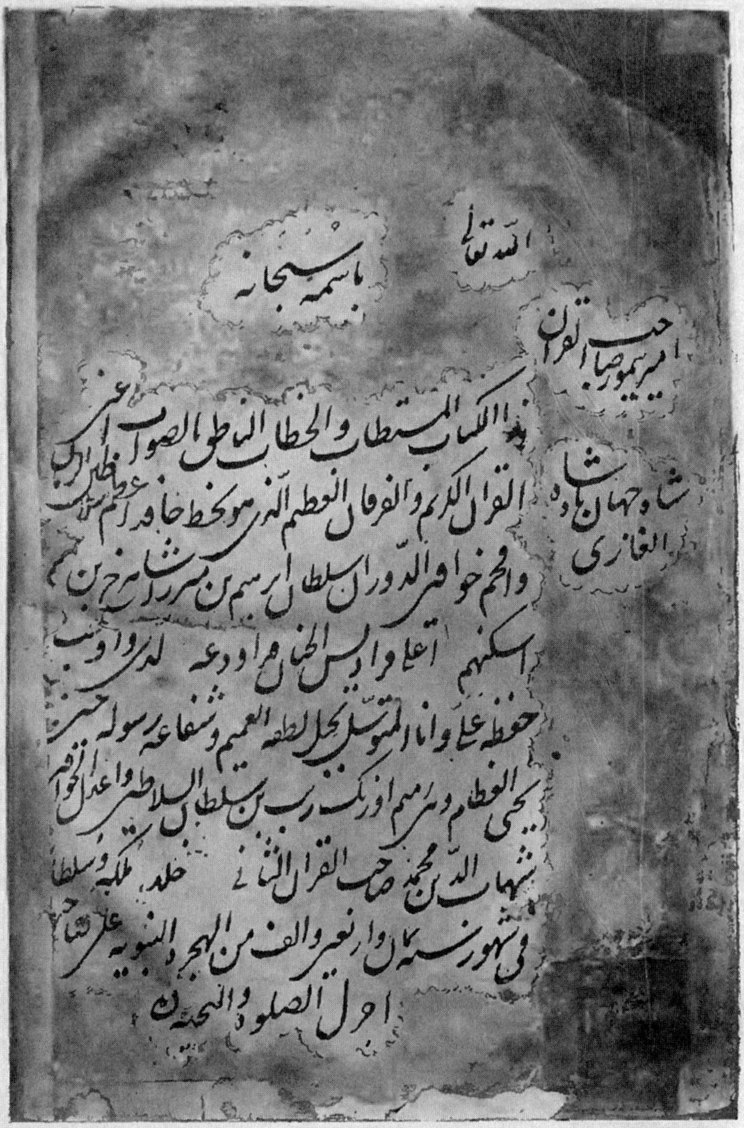

ARABIC MEMORANDUM IN THE HANDWRITING OF THE MUGHAL EMPEROR AURANGZĪB

Ms. No. 24, fol. 268*b* (see page 174)

INDEX

INDEX

In the alphabetic arrangement of names in this index the prefix *al-* has been disregarded. Dates (A.D.) are given whenever possible to facilitate identification. Names of works are printed in italics.

N

T

U